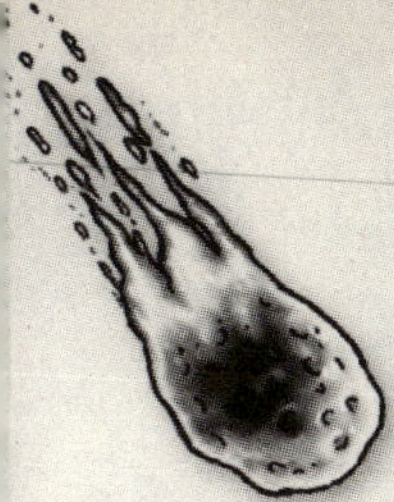

CONTENTS

Anita Ganeri has climbed an erupting volcano, swum through shark-infested oceans and sailed round the world solo. IN HER DREAMS!

But she was born in far-away India, though she didn't realize it at the time. At school, her only interest in geography was staring out of the classroom window and working out how to escape. Since then, Horrible Geography has grown on her a bit like a mould, and she's even learned to read a map without having to turn it upside down.

Mike Phillips was born… Yippee!! No, I mean he was born in London where he grew up and up and eventually got so big he had to leave. Which is when he discovered his love of travelling, and he set off immediately to tour the world. Nearly thirty years later he has reached North Devon where he now illustrates the entire world from a sitting position.

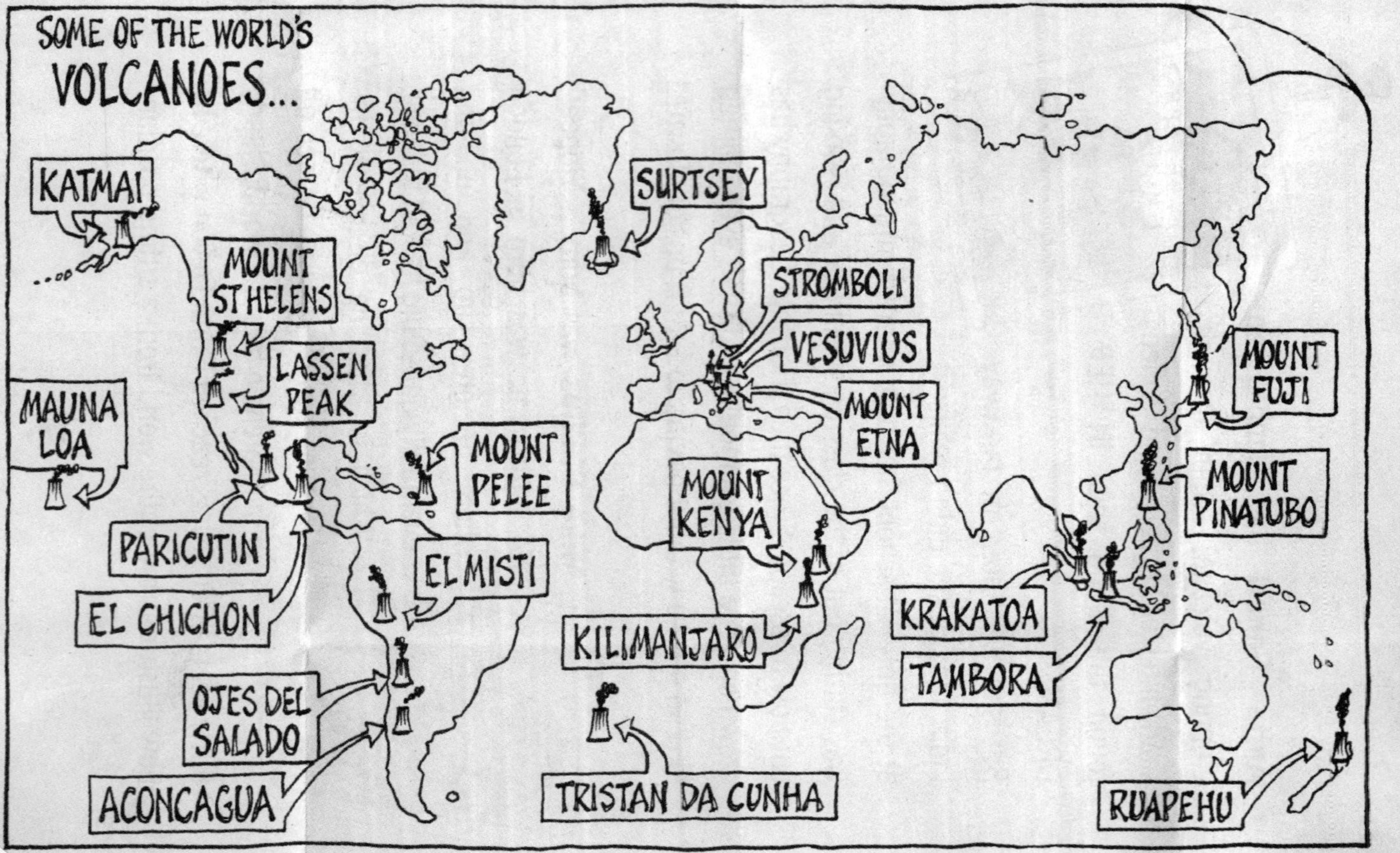
SOME OF THE WORLD'S
VOLCANOES...
KATMAI
MOUNT ST HELENS
LASSEN PEAK
MAUNA LOA
PARICUTIN
EL CHICHON
MOUNT PELEE
EL MISTI
OJES DEL SALADO
ACONCAGUA
SURTSEY
STROMBOLI
VESUVIUS
MOUNT ETNA
MOUNT KENYA
KILIMANJARO
TRISTAN DA CUNHA
KRAKATOA
TAMBORA
MOUNT FUJI
MOUNT PINATUBO
RUAPEHU

INTRODUCTION

Geography can be horribly boring. I mean, who wants to know about boring old maps and boring old rocks and what boring old farmers grow in their fields?

The best bits of geography are the horrible bits – the bits your teacher's bound to leave out. Try this simple experiment. Jump up and down on the spot.

The earth you live on may feel solid as a boring old rock but underneath it's all warm and wobbly. Red-hot rocks and ghastly gases churn away beneath your feet until, one day, they can't take the pressure any longer and burst to the surface with a bang. This is how you get violent volcanoes, one of the most horribly interesting bits of geography ever. (You might notice the same sort of thing happening with your geography teacher, only on a slightly smaller scale.)

And that's what this book is all about. More powerful than a

nuclear bomb, hotter than the hottest oven, more temperamental than your little brother, when a volcano blows its top, it's brilliant, mind-boggling and a red-hot topic, and it certainly isn't boring! In *Violent Volcanoes*, you can...

- watch a volcano erupt (from a safe distance)

- find out why volcanoes smell of rotten eggs
- learn how to spot an active volcano
- train to be a vile volcanologist ...

and, if all else fails, find out which saint to call on if you need saving from a lethal lava flow. This is geography like never before. And it's horribly exciting.

A VERY VIOLENT VOLCANO

The day a mountain blew apart

It is the morning of 18 May 1980. The dawn is bright and clear over the Cascade Mountains of Washington State, USA. For many months now, the perilous peak of Mount St Helens has been shaken by a series of grumbling earthquakes. Smoke and ash from hundreds of minor explosions have covered the ice-capped mountain in an ugly cloak of black. For weeks, scientists have been monitoring an ominous bulge growing on the volcano's north side – a sure sign that magma deep

below the earth is starting its ground-breaking journey upwards.

As they watch, the bulge keeps growing, relentlessly raising the intense pressure on the gases and magma inside the mountain. Something, surely, will have to give. A dormant volcano, Mount St Helens has not erupted in living memory. Now, after 123 years of silence, this sleeping giant seems to be stirring. To those who watch, it seems almost impossible that this beautiful mountain can be a violent killer. But then, the impossible happens...

At 8.32 am, two scientists fly over Mount St Helens. As they approach the summit, all is calm. Seconds later, the mountain shakes with a huge earthquake, dislodging a massive avalanche of rock and ice. Before their eyes, the whole north side of the mountain completely collapses and races downhill at full pelt. Worse is to come. The landslide releases the immense pressure which has been building up inside the mountain. Suddenly, the bulge bursts apart, upwards, outwards and sideways, blasting out a thick, black cloud of hot gas, ash and rock many kilometres into the air. The summit of Mount St Helens is completely shattered.

The scientists have to act fast; the blast cloud is starting to bear down on them. They dive away to the south to safety. The cloud starts expanding to the east, north and north-west, at a speed that could easily overtake their small aircraft. Heading south they are safe for now, but any other direction would mean certain death.

Behind them, the sky turns black as night. Thick showers of ash fall like black rain from the clouds and brilliant bolts of lightning shoot many kilometres into the air. For the next nine hours Mount St Helens continues to erupt, onlookers feel they've had a glimpse of Hell. By evening, the worst explosions are over, but the volcano continues to erupt more gently for four more days. Then at last it falls silent.

One week later, there is another large eruption, several smaller ones follow, but the main force is spent. Mount St Helens has blown its top. Things will never be the same again.

Ten earth-shattering facts about Mount St Helens

1 Before the 1980 eruption, Mount St Helens stood 2,975 metres high. The eruption blew an incredible 400 metres off the top, which crashed down the mountainside as 8,000 million tonnes of rock. That's a lot of rock.

2 The land around Mount St Helens had been a national park, popular with anglers, campers and walkers. All this changed for ever on 18 May, in the space of just five to ten minutes.

The searing blast cloud, heavy with hot gas, ash and rock, stripped bare the countryside in its path. Instead of thick, green forests and clear blue lakes lay a barren desert of grey ash. The cloud was so powerful that it uprooted every tree for 31 kilometres around, picking them up and tossing them aside. As a pilot

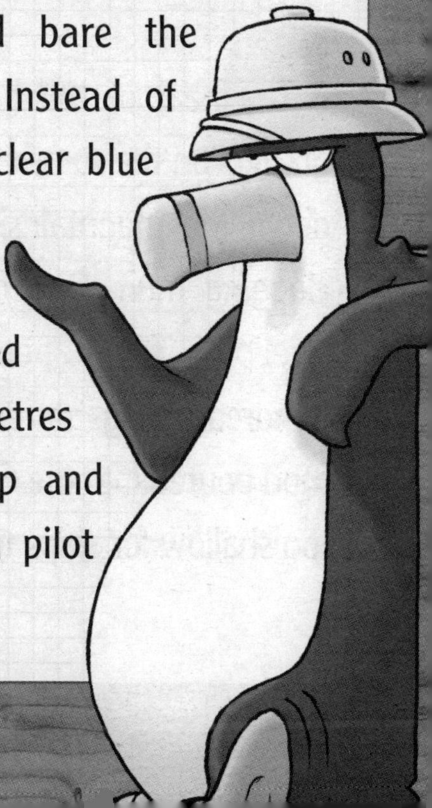

flying overhead reported, it looked as if:

The cloud was so incredibly hot (between 100 and 350°C) that it boiled the sap inside the trees. Wow!

3 The heat of the blast cloud also melted the glaciers on the summit. Ash and meltwater poured down the mountainside in great, thick rivers of clogging mud. One flowed into the Toutle river, sweeping away people, homes, bridges and hundreds of logs stored at a timber camp. So much mud poured into the Columbia river that it became too shallow for ships to sail and had to stay closed for weeks on end. And the river water became so hot that fish were seen leaping *out* of it!

4 One branch of the awesome avalanche of rocks and ice swept into nearby Spirit Lake, causing waves more than 200 metres high (ten times taller than a house). But most of it raced into the Toutle river at speeds of 100–200 kilometres per hour. It was one of the largest landslides ever recorded.

5 The blast cloud of ash, dust and gas rose 19 kilometres into the air. In two days, it had reached New York. In two weeks, it had travelled right around the world. Ash fell like snow on cities and fields up to 600 kilometres away from the volcano, turning day into night. Airports and roads were closed. In the city of Yakima, 150 kilometres away, the sewage works became clogged with ash and would not work.

6 Mount St Helens began rumbling about two months before its eruption. Warning signs included more than 1,500 small earthquakes which cracked the glaciers on the summit, followed by frequent bursts of steam and ash. Meanwhile, the bulge on its side was growing by two whole metres a day. Everything pointed to a violent eruption. But, when it came, the sheer suddenness and staggering force of the explosion took everyone by surprise.

7 Before the main eruption, hundreds of volcano

watchers had come to see the show. Souvenir stalls sprang up everywhere, selling anything from Mount St Helens T-shirts, to mugs, posters and souvenir samples of ash. Even as late as 31 March, a group of people went by helicopter to the summit and began filming a beer commercial! Even today, you can buy glass Christmas tree decorations made from ash from that dreadful day.

8 Scientists set up a 7-kilometre "red zone" around the mountain to protect people from danger. But it didn't go far enough. Of the 57 people killed that day, all but three were well outside the zone. The dead included campers, sightseers and scientists. One scientist was engulfed by the blast cloud and choked to death as he watched from a ridge 9 kilometres away. A worse death toll was only avoided because the volcano blew so early in the day and it was a Sunday.

9 Incredibly, though this was a horribly violent eruption, Mount St Helens seemed to burst apart with barely a sound. The explosion happened so suddenly that the sounds were quickly carried far away.

10 The eruption of Mount St Helens replaced its scenic snow-capped cone with a crater shaped like a horseshoe. But inside the crater, a new dome is growing. Already as tall as an 80-storey building, it will one day fill the mountain and erupt all over again. The burning question is when?

If you compare Mount St Helens to all the eruptions in the history of the Earth, it wasn't even particularly powerful. An eruption 6,000 times as big once hit Yellowstone Park, USA. When the rock and ash settled, it covered a third of the USA – but that happened about two million years ago, so you might think it doesn't count.

HORRIBLE HOT SPOTS

So, who on earth came up with the name volcano to describe a smouldering mountain that can explode? Well, there are different stories around the world to explain what causes volcanoes, but you can blame the actual name on the ancient Romans and their hot-tempered fire god, Vulcan...

According to legend, Vulcan lived on the island of Vulcano, inside a smouldering mountain.

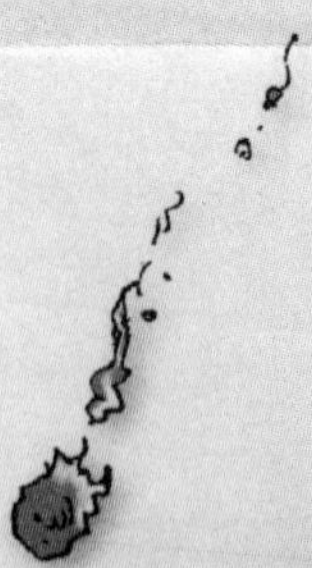

All the smouldering, sparks and rumbling noises were caused byVulcan's frantic activities. He was blacksmith to the gods. He made weapons for Mars...

Armour for Hercules...

And thunderbolts and lightning for Jupiter.

But Vulcan used his skills in other ways too. For no good reason, Vulcan would pick on villagers and terrorize them with fire, lightning, lava flows and explosions!

So, which came first, Vulcan or Vulcano? No one knows, but the name, tweaked a bit, stuck.

What on earth are violent volcanoes?

Ask someone to think of a volcano, and they'll most likely describe a neat cone-shaped mountain, gently breathing smoke. But volcanoes aren't always like that. Volcanoes are all horribly different. Some spurt out fire. Others spew out clouds of steam, gas and ash. Some volcanoes explode with a bang, others fizz quietly away. Some are flat or round or lie deep under the sea.

The best you can say is that all volcanoes are built by red-hot magma (liquid rock) from deep inside the Earth. When it bursts or seeps up through a crack in the ground, you know you're dealing with a volcano!

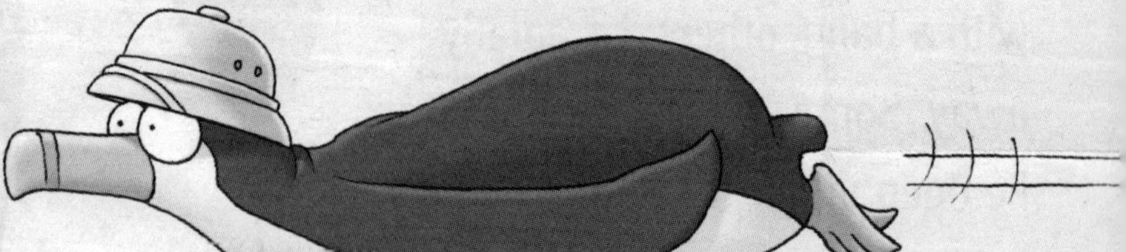

How on earth do volcanoes happen?

To find out, you'll need one Earth (in good condition), with a large-ish chunk cut out. The Earth looks rock solid, feels rock solid and in many places it is rock solid. But not all the way down. The Earth's made of layers, a bit like a big – a really, really big – onion.

You can't see these layers (even your know-all geography teacher can't see them), but these pictures might give you an idea of what they're like.

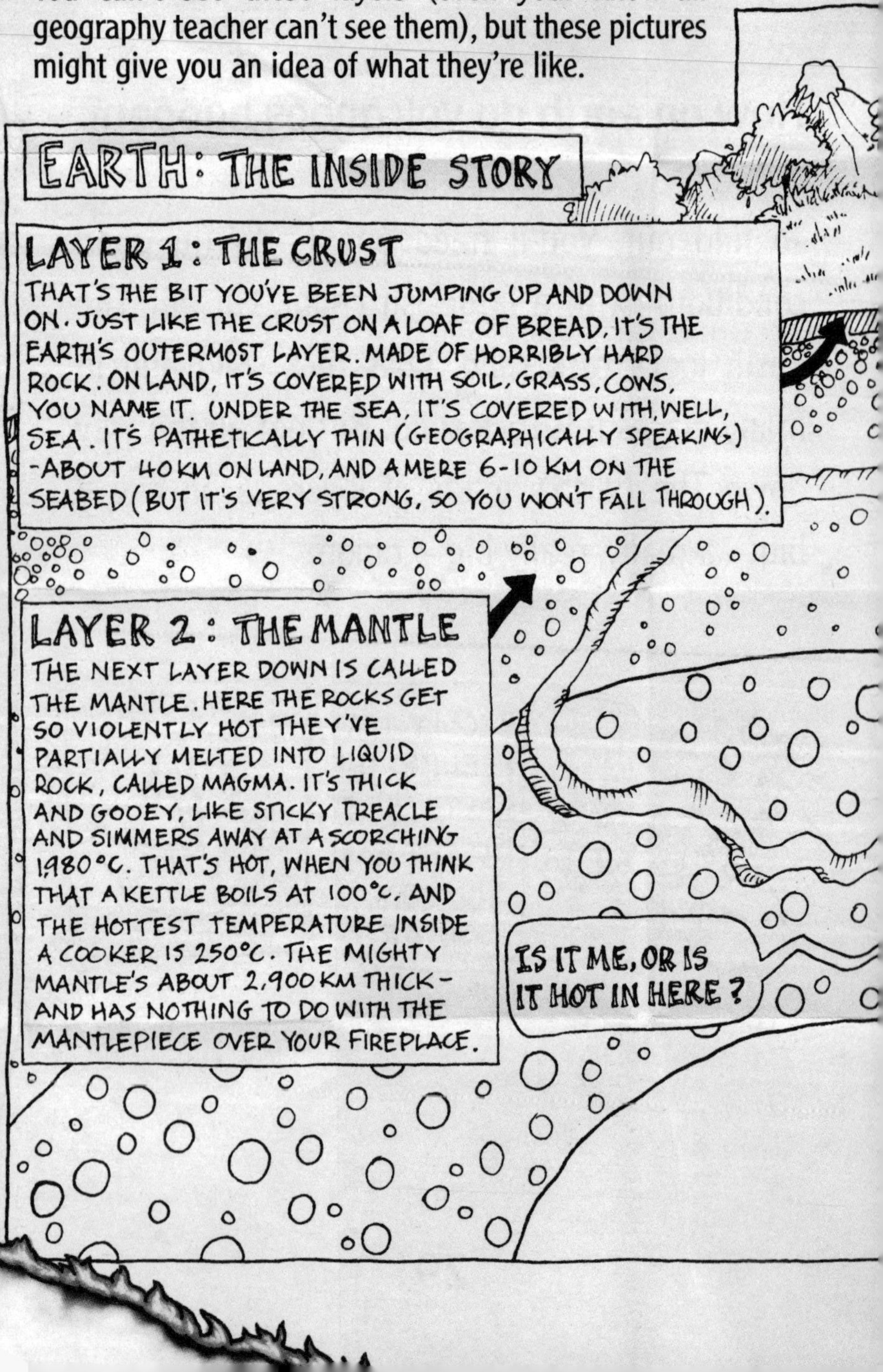

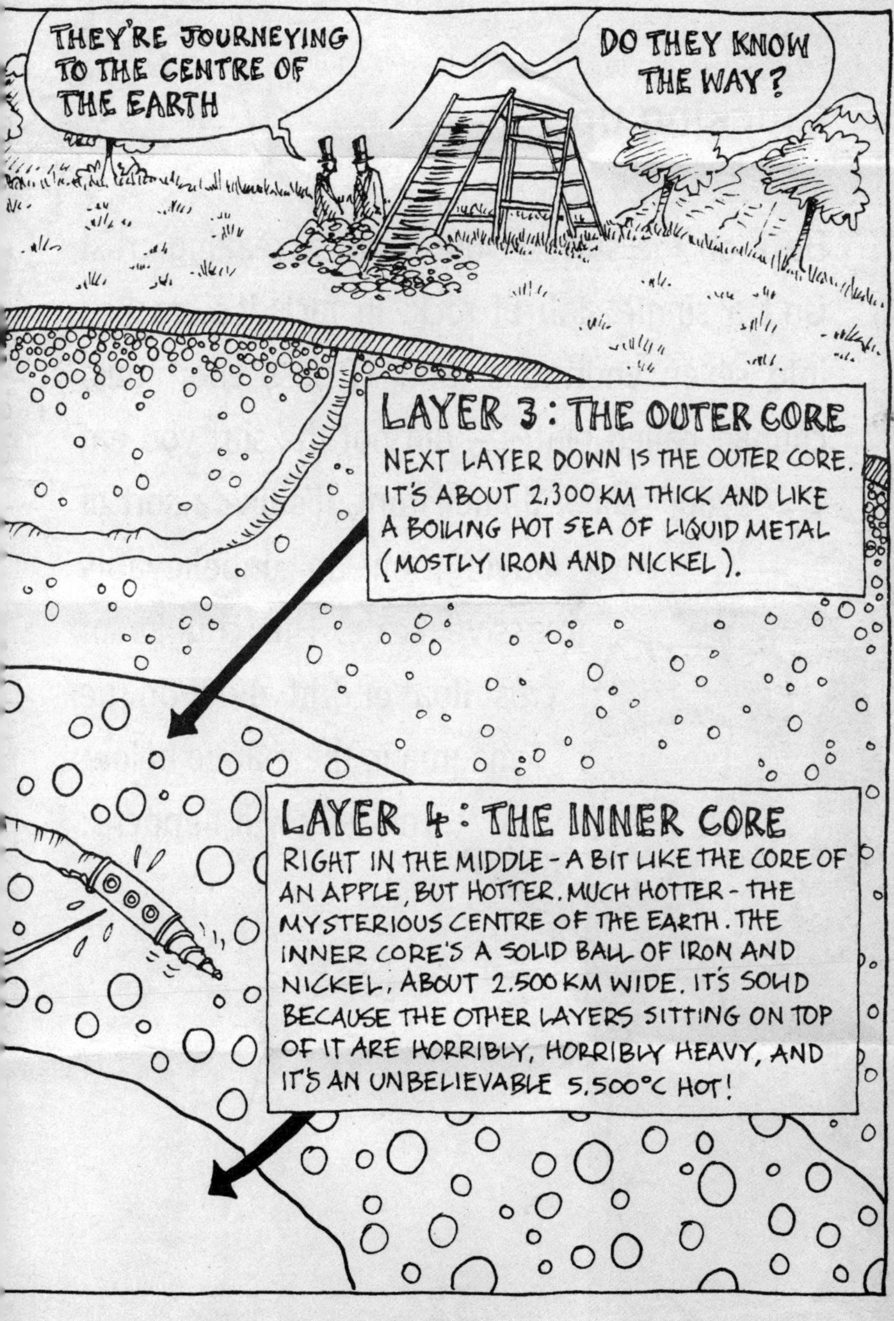
THEY'RE JOURNEYING TO THE CENTRE OF THE EARTH
DO THEY KNOW THE WAY?
LAYER 3: THE OUTER CORE
NEXT LAYER DOWN IS THE OUTER CORE. IT'S ABOUT 2,300 KM THICK AND LIKE A BOILING HOT SEA OF LIQUID METAL (MOSTLY IRON AND NICKEL).
LAYER 4: THE INNER CORE
RIGHT IN THE MIDDLE - A BIT LIKE THE CORE OF AN APPLE, BUT HOTTER. MUCH HOTTER - THE MYSTERIOUS CENTRE OF THE EARTH. THE INNER CORE'S A SOLID BALL OF IRON AND NICKEL, ABOUT 2.500 KM WIDE. IT'S SOLID BECAUSE THE OTHER LAYERS SITTING ON TOP OF IT ARE HORRIBLY, HORRIBLY HEAVY, AND IT'S AN UNBELIEVABLE 5.500°C HOT!

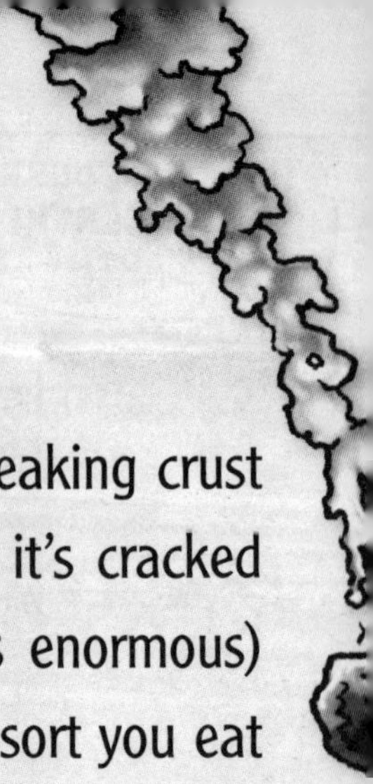

Cracking up

Back on the surface, the Earth's creaking crust isn't a single slab of rock. In fact, it's cracked into seven enormous (and 12 less enormous) chunks, called plates – but not the sort you eat your school dinner from. It's like a sort of crazy paving, on an unbelievably massive scale. The chunks of crust float or drift about on the magma in the mantle below. This is how it happens:

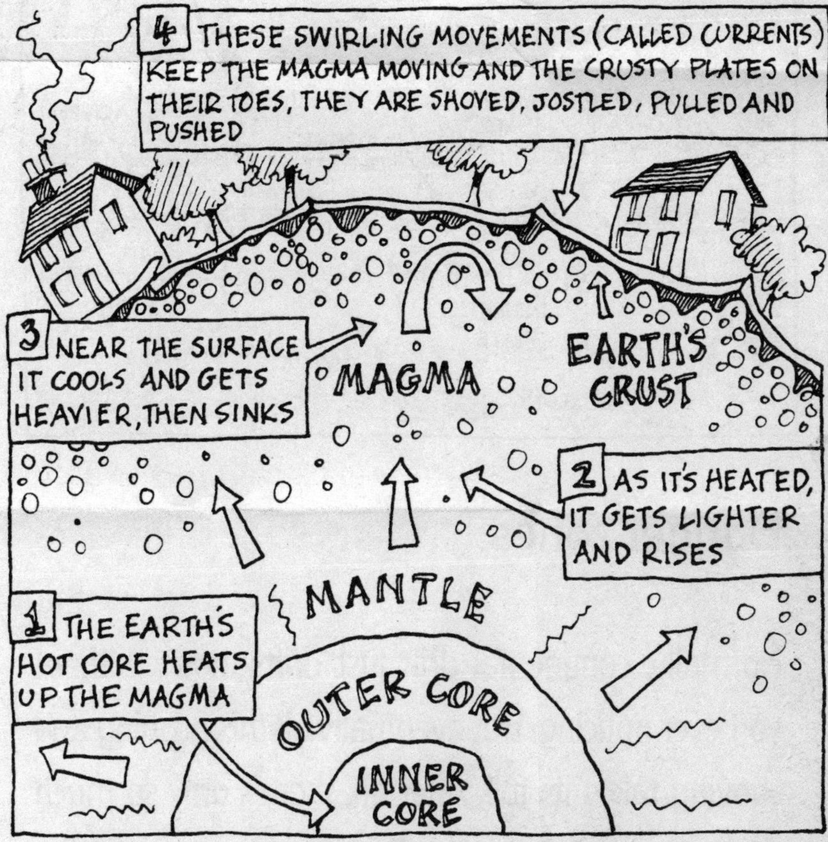

PS To be horribly technical, the way the plates move is called continental drift but you can leave boring details like this to your teacher.

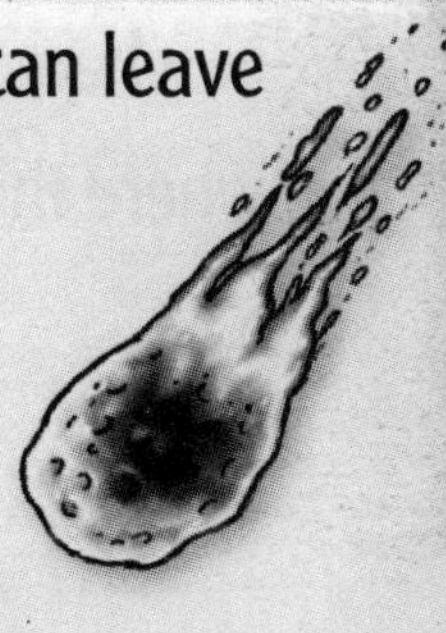

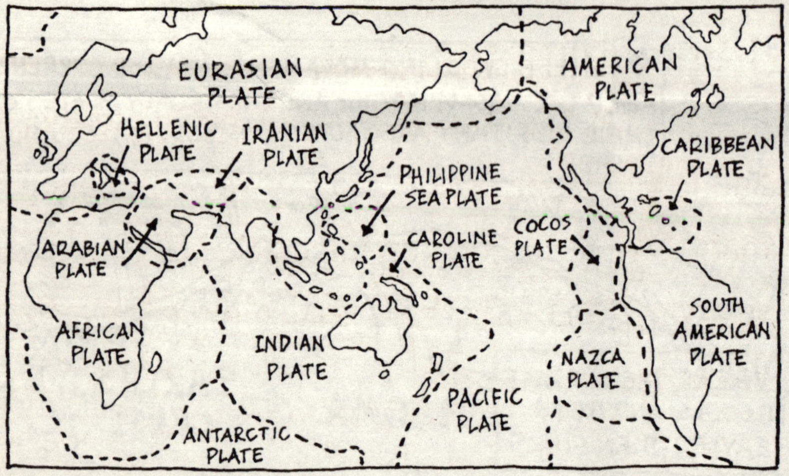

Danger zones

Normally, continental drift just drifts along without you ever noticing. But eventually all this pushing and shoving takes its toll. After all, there's only so much pressure a plate can take. The crumbling crust at the edges of the plates gets weaker and weaker. And this is where volcanoes are born. There are two places where the crust gets particularly weak and wobbly.

1 Spreading sea floor

In some places, two plates are pulled further and further apart. Until … CRAAACK! Bubbling magma wells up through the crack, hits the cold sea water and forms long chains of underwater volcanoes.

Most undersea volcanoes erupt so deep down that – unless you're some sort of deep-sea fish – you don't really notice them. They tend to ooze out lava gently, rather than exploding with a bang. That's nice!

2 Going under

In other places, two plates collide. One plate is dragged down under the other. Deep inside the Earth, it melts into magma, which then rises up through cracks in the crust and erupts as a volcano. These violent volcanoes usually happen along the coast where a crusty plate of seabed is dragged under a crusty plate of land.

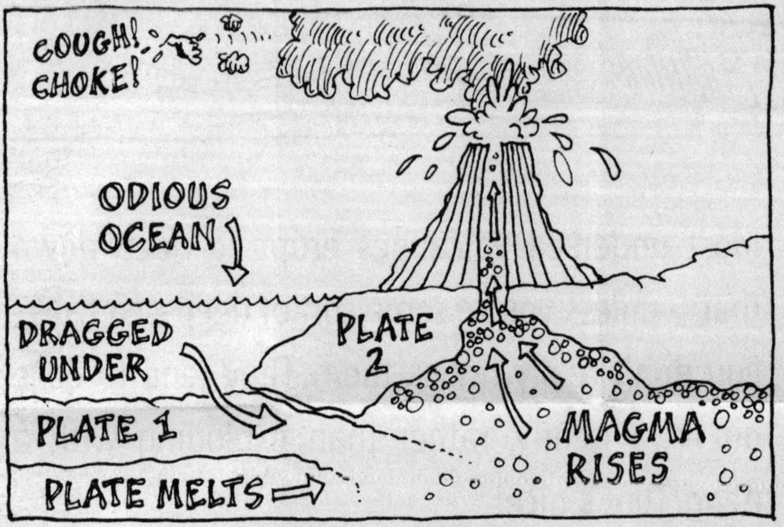

Hot spots

A third type of volcano has nothing to do with drifting continents. It's called a hot spot volcano. To spot a hot spot, you need to look at the middle of a plate where a stream of magma rises up from the mantle. It punches a hole in the crust to form a volcano. Over billions of years, the hot spot stays still but the plate above it crawls slowly over it. As it does so, the old volcanoes die but new holes are punched to make new volcanoes. Slowly, really, really slowly, over millions and millions of years, a chain of volcanoes builds up.

This is how the volcanic islands of exotic Hawaii in the Pacific Ocean came into being.

Earth-shattering fact

And if violent Earth volcanoes weren't enough, what about volcanoes in outer space? At the last count there were 1,728 active volcanoes on violent planet Venus (precisely 228 more than on Earth) and even more on Io, one of Jupiter's moons. Some of these may still be active – scientists can't be sure how many. They spit out plumes of stinking sulphur gas up to 300 kilometres high. Which is pretty good spitting by anyone's standards.

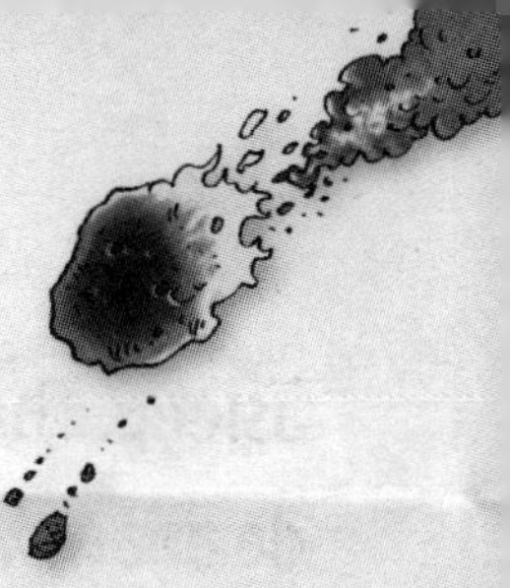

Sleeping beauties

But don't be fooled. One thing to remember about volcanoes is that you can't trust them. Not an inch. Volcanoes are horribly unpredictable.

Officially, volcanoes go through three phases. Though not necessarily in this order. These are:

1 Active – a volcano that is erupting now or has erupted in the past. Some volcanoes are more active than others. Some erupt almost all the time. DON'T PANIC! The last volcano in the UK stopped being active about 50 million years ago. Even teachers can't remember that far back.

2 Dormant – a volcano that isn't erupting now but probably will in the future. Dormant means asleep. That doesn't mean it's not dangerous. A dormant volcano can sleep peacefully for weeks, months and even centuries on end, then suddenly wake up. And generally speaking, the longer it snoozes, the bigger the bang next time.

3 Extinct – a volcano that has stopped erupting and isn't likely to erupt again. A dead volcano. Probably. Even dead, a volcano's dangerous. Take Tristan da Cunha, for example, a volcanic island in the South Atlantic Ocean. Everyone thought it was long extinct, until one day in October 1961, when Tristan da Cunha suddenly blew its top. To escape, the 280 islanders took to the sea in their boats. It was two long years before they were allowed home again.

VIOLENT VOLCANIC FACTS TO TEST YOUR TEACHER

How many violent volcanoes are there on Earth? How big is the biggest ever? Where do most volcanoes erupt? Try this quick-fire quiz to find out. Answer TRUE or FALSE

1 There are about 1,500 active volcanoes on Earth.
2 Most volcanoes erupt at sea.

3 Tristan da Cunha is the most active volcano on Earth.

4 The largest active volcano on Earth is Mount Everest.

5 The biggest volcano in the known universe is Olympus Mons on Mars.

6 The 1980 eruption of Mount St Helens was the deadliest ever known.

7 In 1883, Krakatoa in Indonesia exploded with one of the loudest sounds ever heard.

8 Volcanoes can be as violent as a nuclear bomb. They produce the same amount of energy.

9 If you want to see a volcano, head for Indonesia. It's the most violently volcanic place on Earth.

10 All volcanoes are millions of years old.

ANSWER

1 TRUE. And about 50 of them erupt every year. More than half lie clustered in the "Ring of Fire" which loops around the Pacific Ocean. Here the sea floor is being dragged under the land.

2 TRUE. Only about a third of all active volcanoes bubble away on land. The rest are hidden underwater, along with a million others which are dormant or extinct. Sometimes underwater volcanoes grow so tall, their heads poke up above the waves and form islands.

3 FALSE. Kilauea, Hawaii, is much more active than that. It has erupted non-stop since 1983 and has several craters, not just one. The one that started erupting in 1983 is called Pu'u O'o. Since the eruptions started the island of Hawaii has gained an extra 2 square kilometres of new land – that's about the same as 184 football pitches.

4 FALSE. The record-holder is Mauna Loa in Hawaii. It measures 120 kilometres across and stands 9,000 metres from the ocean floor as an awesome island. Mount Everest only stands 8,848 metres tall. And it isn't even a volcano.

5 TRUE. Olympus Mons stands 27 kilometres high, three times taller than Mauna Loa (see above), and is an incredible 650 kilometres in diameter. At the top is a crater as big as a city. This voluminous volcano last erupted about 200 million years ago and is now extinct – luckily for any Martians.

6 FALSE. The worst eruption of recent times was that of Tambora, Indonesia in 1815. It threw out more than 150 cubic kilometres of ash, lowering the island more than a kilometre. 92,000 people died. This eruption was 100 times more violent than that of Mount St Helens.

7 TRUE. This amazing explosion was heard in Australia, a staggering 3,500 kilometres away. Ear-witnesses said it sounded like heavy gunfire. And the shock was felt 14,500 kilometres away in California, USA.

8 FALSE. The energy produced by Mount St Helens in 1980 was equal to 500 nuclear bombs, not one. Truly awesome energy.

9 TRUE. Indonesia has more than its fair share of active volcanoes, about 125 in all. That's because it lies on the edges of several different plates of crust and in the Ring of Fire. Runner-up is Japan, with the USA in third place.

10 FALSE. It's true that some volcanoes are horribly old (at a million years old a volcano is still in its prime), but there are some real youngsters around. The youngest volcano on land is Parícutin in Mexico which erupted in 1943. A mere baby in volcanic terms. Amazingly, a Mexican farmer witnessed Parícutin's birth. Now there's something you don't see every day. This is what happened...

The Volcano that grew in a Field

On the morning of 20 February, 1943, farmer, Dionisio Pulido, ploughs his field of corn, in the village of Paricutin, Mexico...

The terrified farmer leaps on his horse and gallops for cover.
FASTER!
THAT EVENING
The crack has grown into a large hole, red-hot rocks, ash and cinders shoot into the air, flashes of lightning streak across the sky. Every few seconds the ground shakes.
NEXT DAY
Overnight the volcano erupts non-stop and its cone grows 50 metres high. And it's still growing, hour by hour...
BY THE END OF THE WEEK
The cone now stands at 150 metres high. It erupts violently, shooting balls of fire high into the sky. Farmer Dionisio packs his bags as lava destroys his village.

Parícutin gave geographers a brilliant opportunity to study a violent volcano first-hand. But volcanoes still remain horribly mysterious. And horribly difficult to predict. So what exactly is it that makes a volcano tick?

GOING OUT WITH A BANG!

While you're sneaking a snooze in your geography lesson, or vegging out in front of the telly, spare a thought for the poor old Earth. Beneath your feet, the energetic Earth never gets a moment's rest. It's always on the go. And it's this earthly activity that causes volcanoes. The burning question is how?

How on earth do volcanoes erupt?

1 Deep underground in the mantle, magma rises upwards. It rises because it's mixed with gas so it's lighter than the rocks around it. To see how magma rises, try this edible experiment:

What you will need:

- two corks (for the magma)
- a jar of honey (for the rocks)

What you do:

a) Push the corks into the honey so they are completely covered.

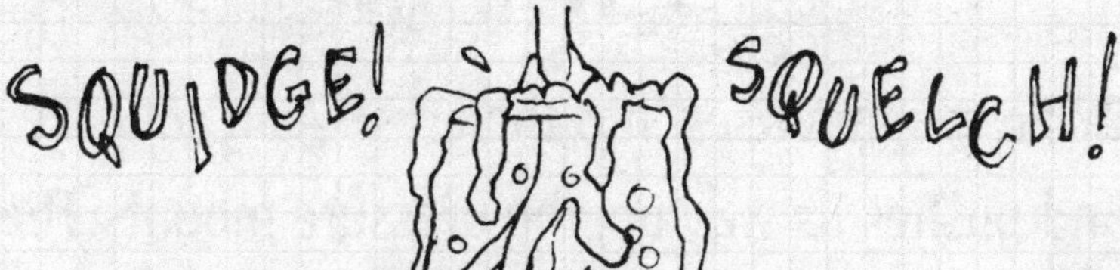

b) Watch them bob upwards. Just like magma (well, almost).

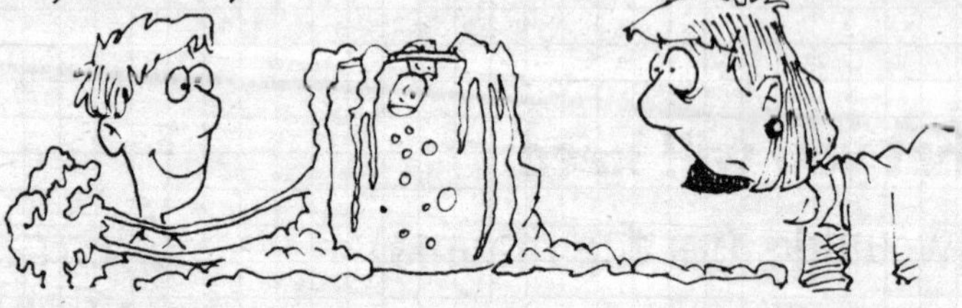

c) Spread the honey on toast and eat it. (Take the corks out first.)

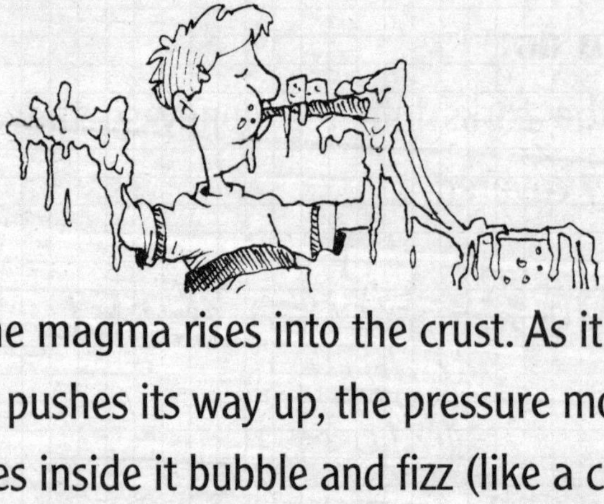

2 The magma rises into the crust. As it squeezes and pushes its way up, the pressure mounts. The gases inside it bubble and fizz (like a can of pop if you shake it). The pressure goes up…

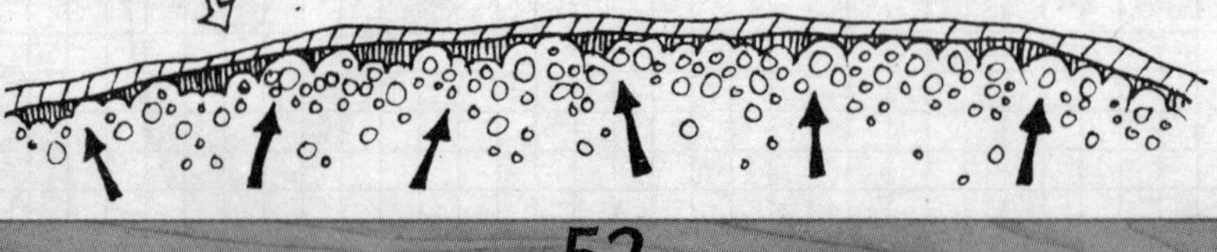

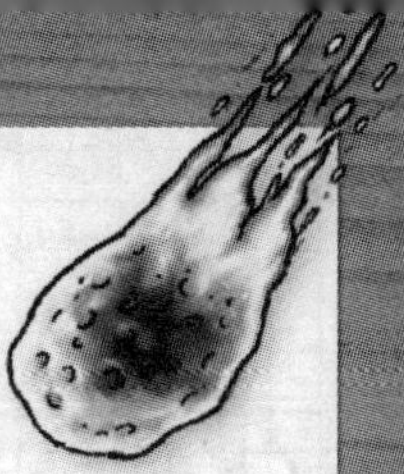

3 And up ... and up.

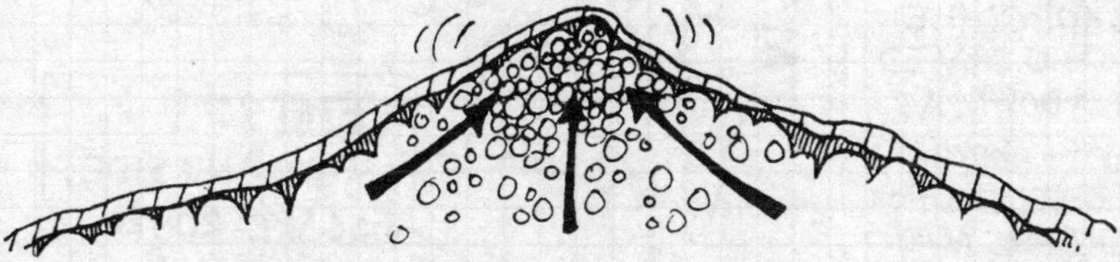

4 ... until, one day, the magma and gas rush upwards, burst out through cracks in the crust, and erupt. (As the pop will when you open the can, so be warned.)

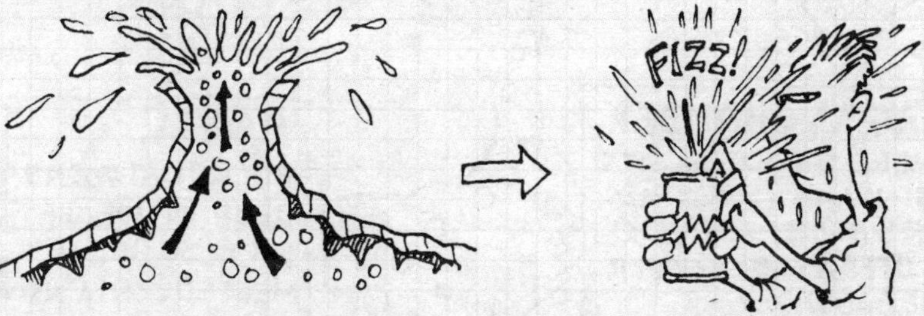

5 Above the ground, magma's called lava. It's red-hot, sticky and in a hurry. It bursts out with a bang or oozes out steadily, building a cone or creeping across the ground. Eventually, it cools and becomes solid cold rock.

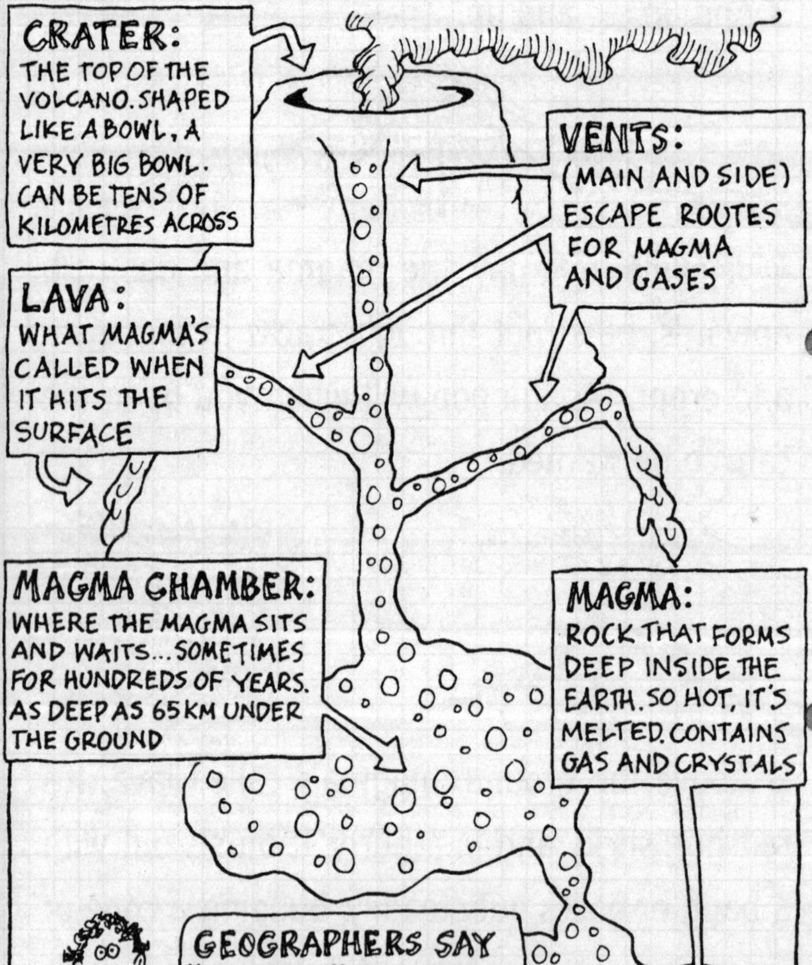
CRATER:
THE TOP OF THE VOLCANO. SHAPED LIKE A BOWL, A VERY BIG BOWL. CAN BE TENS OF KILOMETRES ACROSS
VENTS:
(MAIN AND SIDE) ESCAPE ROUTES FOR MAGMA AND GASES
LAVA:
WHAT MAGMA'S CALLED WHEN IT HITS THE SURFACE
MAGMA CHAMBER:
WHERE THE MAGMA SITS AND WAITS... SOMETIMES FOR HUNDREDS OF YEARS. AS DEEP AS 65 KM UNDER THE GROUND
MAGMA:
ROCK THAT FORMS DEEP INSIDE THE EARTH. SO HOT, IT'S MELTED. CONTAINS GAS AND CRYSTALS
GEOGRAPHERS SAY "MOLTEN" INSTEAD OF "MELTED." BUT IT'S JUST SHOWING OFF
NIK

All shapes and sizes

Needless to say, not all volcanoes are shaped like this. It all depends on exactly what type of magma they're made from (thick or thin) and exactly how violently they erupt. There are usually two main types of eruption – 1 incredibly violent and 2 not so very violent (Vic's descriptions, not official).

TYPES OF VOLCANIC ERUPTION – REPORT

① Incredibly Violent (IV, for short)

Some volcanoes really go with a Bang! Like the mega-eruption of Mount St Helens.

The magma that causes very violent volcanoes is thick and sticky, and highly charged with gas. It bursts to the surface in a violent explosion, blasting boiling-hot clouds of rock, ash and gases into the sky.

Verdict: Dreadful, destructive and dangerous to know.

② Not very violent (NVV, for short)

If magma is thin and runny, gases escape from it easily, so any eruption is much less violent.

Lava oozes gently from the ground and flows away in streams. And it can flow for miles, burning and burying everything in its path. They also produce fabulous firework displays, spraying sparkling fountains of lava high into the air.

Verdict: Silent-ish, but deadly.

Of course, there are always exceptions to every rule. Some volcanoes start off life as one type and end up as another. Some erupt in both ways at the same time. Phew!

Earth-shattering fact

All that huffing and blowing takes its toll so some volcanoes sneak a short rest between eruptions. Stromboli in Italy erupts quite gently most of the time. In between each small eruption it only has a 15–20 minute breather – so it could be erupting as you read this fact. El Chichon in Mexico takes a bit longer. It slumbers away for hundreds of years between eruptions. Just to keep you guessing.

Spotter's guide to volcanoes

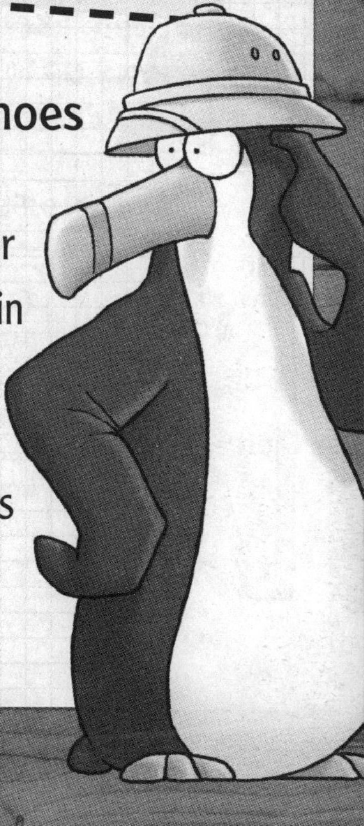

- Can't tell your shields from your cones? Getting your magmas in a muddle? Help is at hand! With this sizzling new spotter's guide, your worries will soon be over.

Ⓐ NAME: Shield volcano
SHAPE: Low, wide and dome shaped

MAGMA/LAVA RATING: Thin and runny, like hot syrup. Fast moving. Flows up to 100 km before it hardens.

ERUPTION TYPE: NVV

The shield volcano is named after a warrior's shield. (Can <u>you</u> spot the difference?) They build the largest mountains on earth. Lots of side vents for lava to flow from. Kilauea, Mauna Loa and the three other volcanoes which make up the idyllic islands of Hawaii, are all famous examples.

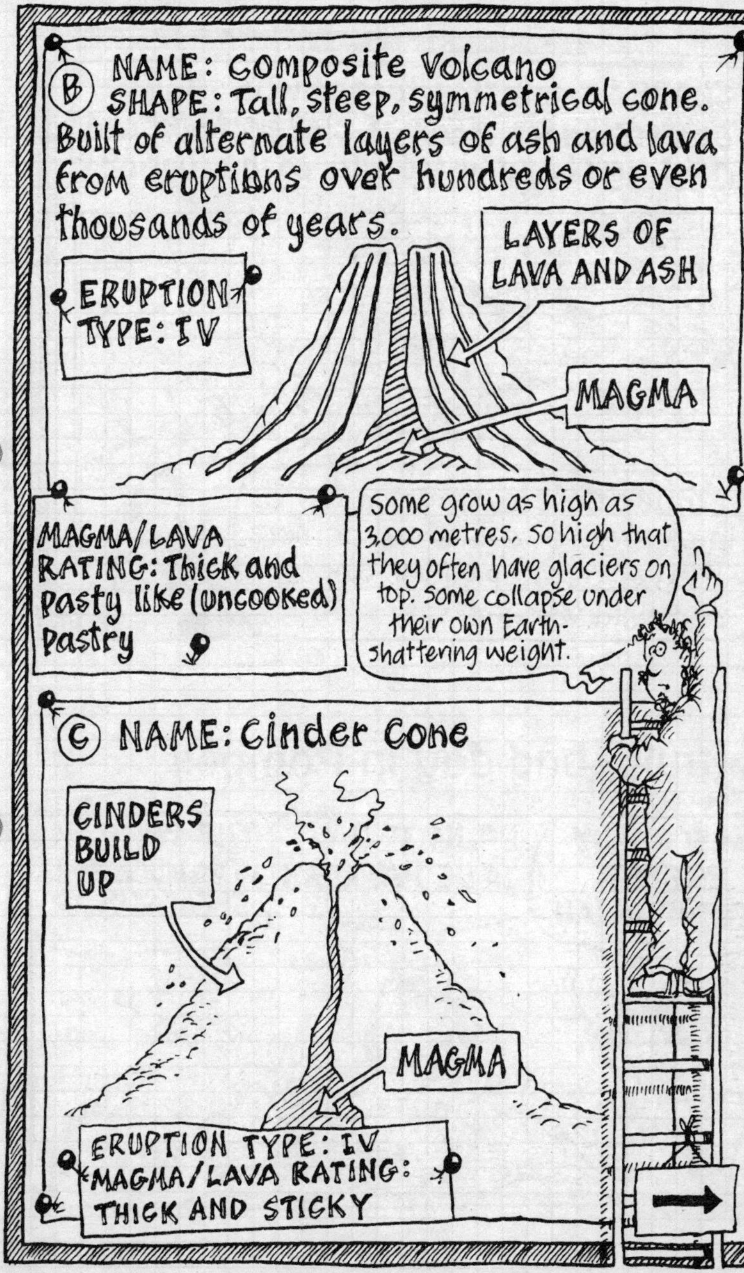
B NAME: Composite volcano
SHAPE: Tall, steep, symmetrical cone.
Built of alternate layers of ash and lava from eruptions over hundreds or even thousands of years.
LAYERS OF LAVA AND ASH
ERUPTION TYPE: IV
MAGMA
MAGMA/LAVA RATING: Thick and pasty like (uncooked) pastry
Some grow as high as 3,000 metres, so high that they often have glaciers on top. Some collapse under their own Earth-shattering weight.
C NAME: Cinder Cone
CINDERS BUILD UP
MAGMA
ERUPTION TYPE: IV
MAGMA/LAVA RATING: THICK AND STICKY

A (truly) bad day in Pompeii

Well, they're not talking about their pizzas. What else would you expect three volcanologists to discuss over dinner? Yup, they're talking about types of volcanic eruption. The names come from:

- Strombolian after the Stromboli volcano in Italy.
- Hawaiian after the Hawaiian volcanoes (which is horribly misleading since Iceland's volcanoes are also Hawaiian!).
- Plinian, after Pliny the Elder. He was a Roman nobleman and writer (with a special interest in geography!) who died when Mount Vesuvius erupted in 79 CE and buried the town of Pompeii in ash.

Plinian volcanoes are the most violent volcanoes of all. Luckily (for us), the eruption was witnessed first-hand (though from a safe distance) by Pliny's 18-year-old nephew, Pliny the Younger. He wrote about the dramatic events in a letter to a friend. It was the first ever eyewitness account of a violent volcanic eruption. Here's a very, very rough translation!

> Naples, Italy
> AD 79
>
> Dear Tacitus,
>
> I'm sorry I haven't written for ages. Thanks very much for the history books you sent for my birthday. I'm just finishing 'A Beginners' Guide to Gladiators', then I'll start yours. Things have been pretty grim since I wrote to you last, what with Mount Vesuvius erupting and everything. You probably heard all about it in the news but Mum and I were actually there!

We were staying with Uncle Pliny in Misenum just across the bay where Uncle Pliny was having a few days off. He'd just been made admiral of the fleet and I think work was getting him down a bit. Anyway, it was just after lunch, when Mum suddenly pointed at the sky – at the biggest, blackest cloud you've ever seen.

Uncle Pliny had dozed off in the sun – we had to shake him awake, but when he saw the cloud he put on his shoes and shot up the hill to get a better look. Mum and I hurried after him. The cloud was huge. It looked a bit like a pine tree, you know the ones that look like umbrellas that grow near our house? It was blotchy and dirty, like an old rag, and it was hanging right over Mount Vesuvius! Uncle Pliny started to get all serious, and said that in the interest of science, he ought to go and see what was going on for himself. (If the volcano was really erupting, he wasn't missing out.)

So he called for a boat (you can if you've just been made an admiral) to take him across the bay. He asked me if I wanted to go with him. "You'll learn something new, young Pliny," he said. But I said I'd stay at home, and take care of Mum (not that she needed looking after - funnily enough, I didn't really fancy coming face-to-face with an erupting volcano.)

Just as Uncle was leaving, a letter arrived, marked urgent. It was from his friend, Rectina, who lived right on the slopes of Vesuvius. She begged my Uncle to come and rescue her. The only way to escape from her house was by boat. So Uncle Pliny, always a gentleman, changed his plans and gave orders for a warship to be launched (yet another admiral's perk). He'd save Rectina and anyone else he could find.

Well, we never saw Uncle Pliny again. We heard, some time later, that he'd sailed straight into the danger zone (he always was a bit of a show off)

while everyone was running away. And by the time he got there, thick, hot ash was falling from the sky, followed by great lumps of pumice and rock. Most people would have run for their lives, but Uncle Pliny was there in the interest of science, so he started taking notes. (Well, he didn't actually write them himself. He was far too busy giving orders. No, he had a scribe do all his writing - poor bloke probably wished he'd never learnt to write.)

Anyway, to cut a long story short, it was too dangerous to land near Rectina's house, so the ship sailed to nearby Stabiae, where Uncle's great friend, Pomponianus, lived. (Rectina did escape, you'll be pleased to know. She wrote saying she was sorry to hear of Uncle's death. She must be feeling pretty guilty!)

Meanwhile, Vesuvius was erupting like mad, it felt like the end of the world. The earth was shaking and it got too dangerous for Uncle to stay in Pomponianus's house, so they tied some pillows on their heads, to protect them from falling rocks, and set off for the shore, hoping to make their escape by sea.

But the sea was too choppy to launch the boat. Even Uncle must have been frightened but he didn't let on (he never liked to worry others). He lay down to rest and, someone said, he kept asking a slave for a drink of water.

Soon they could smell burning, there was a fire nearby, and it was getting closer. Uncle Pliny struggled to his feet and tried to walk away. But he couldn't make it. Suddenly, he collapsed and fell to the ground. He couldn't breathe because the fumes were so thick.

They found Uncle's body two days later. The man who found him said he looked like someone asleep rather than someone who had just died, so hopefully he didn't suffer too much.

Mum's been very brave about it but I know she misses Uncle very much. So do I, even though he always found a reason to tell me off. At least he died a hero. Others died too. Have you heard about Pompeii? We saw it last week. There's nothing left at all. Nothing!

Sorry this letter's been so gloomy. Come and see us soon.

Yours Pliny

Five fiery facts about Pompeii

1 In the first century CE, Pompeii was a large, well-off Roman town near Naples, Italy. Twenty thousand people lived there. The poet, Florus, described it as...

2 Mount Vesuvius had been dormant for 800 years and most people thought it was extinct. No one dreamt it would suddenly wake up. Many people didn't even know it was a volcano.

3 According to Pliny, the eruption began at 10 am on 24 August 79 CE. Within a few short hours, Pompeii had been buried under several metres of hot ash and rock, leaving no trace of the town.

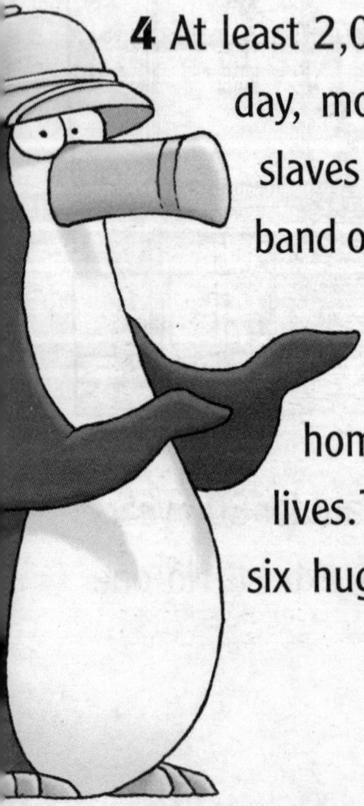

4 At least 2,000 people died on that fateful day, most from the intense heat. Ten slaves died together, crossing a roof. A band of gladiators perished in a tavern. Hundreds of people were trapped in the ruins of their homes. Many more fled for their lives. Those who died were caught by six huge blasts of ash and gas that rolled relentlessly down the mountainside. It must have been terrifying.

5 Geographers use the word Plinian to describe volcanic eruptions like the one that destroyed Pompeii. Their especially violent features include an enormous blast of gas lasting from a few hours to several days, which shoots out huge amounts of rock and ash. This eventually falls, like a sinister, suffocating snowstorm.

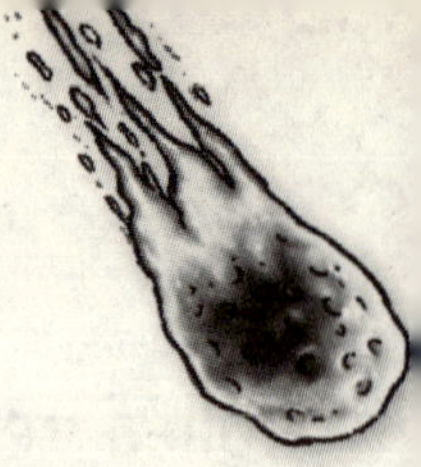

Violent and deadly

Devastating and deadly though it was, in the top ten worst ever violent volcanoes, Vesuvius hardly rates as violent at all. In geographical time (which is much, much longer than normal time. Is that why geography lessons seem to last so long?), Mount Vesuvius wasn't even that bad. To get an idea of exactly how violent a volcano is, scientists use the Volcanic Explosivity Index (VEI for short), with grades from 0 (gentle) to 8 (cataclysmic). The biggest recent eruption was Tambora, Indonesia, in 1815. It scored a 7 on the scale. (Incredibly, Mount St Helens only scored 5.) The modern world has never experienced a VEI 8 eruption.

Check out the chart opposite for a terrifying top ten of the world's most violent eruptions over the last 7,000 years. In order of age, they are:

VOLCANO/LOCATION	DATE	VEI
10) Crater Lake, USA,	4895, BCE VEI	7
9) Kikai, Japan,	4350, BCE VEI	7
8) Taupo, New Zealand,	186, VEI	7
7) Baitoushan, China,	c.1050, VEI	7
6) Long Island, New Guinea,	c.1660, VEI	6
5) Tambora, Indonesia,	1815, VEI	7
4) Krakatau, Indonesia,	1883, VEI	6
3) Santa Maria, Guatemala,	1902, VEI	6
2) Novarupta, Alaska,	1912, VEI	6
1) Pinatubo, Philippines,	1991, VEI	6

Earth-shattering fact

The last VEI 8 eruption was Toba, Sumatra, 75,000 years ago. This gigantic explosion pumped so much ash and gas into the atmosphere that it completely blocked out the Sun. Temperatures plummeted and the Earth was gripped by a freezing volcanic winter which lasted for years and years. DONT PANIC! Really violent eruptions are much rarer than smaller ones because it takes much longer to build up the pressure needed to make a really big bang.

Awesome ash ratings

Another way of estimating the earth-shattering size of an eruption is to measure the amount of ash belched out. (Be warned, this could take some time!) For example, temperamental old Toba (with its VEI score of 8) threw up 2,800 cubic kilometres of ash. That's a thousand times more than Mount St Helens which produced a pathetic 2.5 cubic kilometres. Chart-topping Pinatubo hit the number one spot in 1991 (with a VEI score of 6). It blasted out 5 cubic kilometres of ash, more than double that of Mount St Helens. And if you bear in mind that it only takes one paltry cubic kilometres of ash to fill half a million Olympic-sized swimming-pools, we're talking awesome amounts of ash.

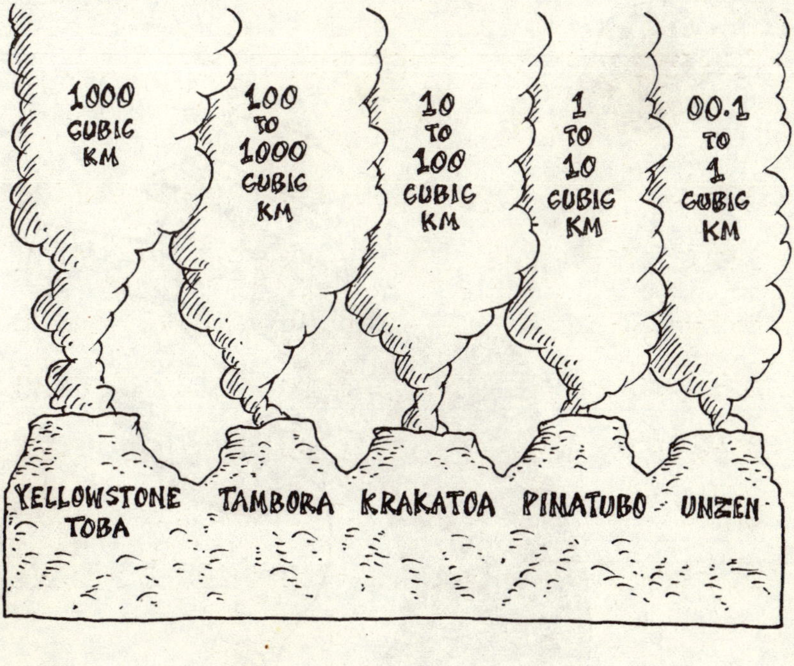

But awesome ash isn't the only thing that comes out of violent volcanoes. They've got a whole range of sinister surprises churning away in their red-hot insides.

SPIT IT OUT

The most horribly dangerous thing about volcanoes is not what goes in but what comes out. There's lava, of course, and lots more besides. Red-hot rocks the size of cars, murky mudflows, smouldering showers of ash and cinders, even fish. That's right, fish!

All the things thrown out of volcanoes (except the fish) are called pyroclasts, a posh Greek word for 'fiery bits'. And they can be killers. Here are some horrible hazards you might want to avoid:

Lively lava

Lava is red-hot, liquid rock from inside the Earth that erupts from a volcano. (Before this, it's called magma.) In not-so very-violent volcanoes, it oozes out gently and flows slowly downhill like a red-hot river of rock. In more explosive eruptions, it bursts out in fiery fountains or blasts out in great globules of goo. When lava cools, it looks completely different and turns into hard black rock.

Ten flaming facts about lava

1 Liquid lava is hair-raisingly hot. It's never cooler than 800°C and can reach a sizzling 1,200°C. That's 12 times hotter than boiling water. A scientist who (unwisely) walked on top of a lava flow still had smoking socks when he took his boots off several hours later!

2 Lava rarely flows faster than a few kilometres an hour so there's normally time to escape. But speed isn't everything. Once lava gets going, nothing can stop it. It grinds along, like a gigantic bulldozer, burying roads, cars, even whole villages, and setting fire to houses and trees.

3 The fastest-ever lava flow leaked out of a lake on Nyirangongo volcano in the Democratic Republic of Congo in 1977. Racing along at over 100 kilometres an hour, it caught local people by surprise. Tragically, hundreds were killed.

4 If you can't beat the lava, get out of its way. When a lava flow threatened the town of Kalapana in Hawaii in 1983, people took drastic action. They hoisted their houses (and local church) on to the back of lorries and moved them away to safety. Behind them, the town burned to the ground.

5 The longest lava flow in recent times poured out of Laki volcano in Iceland, in 1783. It flowed for a distance of 70 kilometres before grinding to a halt.

6 The longest-lasting lava flow comes from Kilauea, Hawaii. It has been erupting non-stop since 1983, and is still going strong. The eruption's wrecked loads of nearby homes and buildings, including the visitor centre.

7 Talking of Kilauea, this is the volcano which Pele, the Hawaiian goddess of fire, calls home, sweet home. She lives in a crater on the summit. The fine, glassy strands of lava which are blown out of the volcano when it erupts are known as Pele's hair.

8 When lava oozes out of the ground, it sounds like a steam train, chugging merrily along. It may even go through tunnels. Sometimes the top of a lava flow sets solid while liquid lava still flows inside. When the lava's gone, a tube or tunnel is left. There's a whole maze of them under honeycombed Hawaii.

9 The nastiest fact about lava is that it can chug along for years and years, then suddenly stop … and then suddenly start again. So you never know quite where you are.

10 If you're off to the beach on a volcanic island, don't be bamboozled by the jet black sand. This forms when hot lava hits the sea and is shattered into billions of tiny specks. You may not have the beach to yourself. The maleo bird from Indonesia uses the black sand as a nest, burying its eggs in the sand. Here, they're kept wonderfully warm and snug until the chicks hatch out.

Violently funny volcanologist's joke

A pillow lava is a type of lava which comes from underwater volcanoes. It billows out of cracks in the seabed, cools very quickly in the cold water and solidifies into rocky blobs. Watch out if you're thinking of snuggling up to a piece of pillow lava. It's not soft, or comfy.

Awful ash

Lava's not the only horrible hazard from volcanoes. Some violent volcanoes blast out clouds of choking, clogging red-hot ash and dust, tens of kilometres into the air. The ash is made of superfine fragments of lava and rock, like chalk or flour, and there's millions and millions of tonnes of it. Some of it's carried far away. Some settles closer to home. And, that's when problems begin. It buries towns and fields for miles around, making it horribly hard even to breathe.

When Japan's Mount Unzen suddenly erupted in 1991,

even the street lights were fooled when a vast cloud of ash blotted out the sun, turning day to night in towns all around. So fooled, they all came on. But if they thought that was bad, they probably hadn't reckoned on the…

Perilous pyroclastic flows

Without doubt, the worst hazards of all from volcanoes are pyroclastic flows. These happen when an ash cloud collapses, and pours and rolls down the mountainside like a glowing, ashy, gassy avalanche, hugging the ground and sweeping rocks and trees away. For anything in the killer flow's path, there is NO ESCAPE. Pyroclastic flows are…

1 FAST! Travelling at up to 720 kilometres an hour!
2 HOT – from 300°C to 800°C, or even hotter!
3 and DEADLY! A pyroclastic flow from the 1902 eruption of Mount Pelée in Martinique demolished the island's capital city and suffocated its 30,000 inhabitants in a matter of seconds…

It was a series of deadly pyroclastic flows that did for Pompeii in 79 CE. But, strangely, they also saved the town for posterity. By covering the town in a thick layer of ash, it was kept in almost perfect condition until archaeologists unearthed it centuries later. Even down to some ancient Roman loaves of bread.

A more grisly discovery was a group of bodies, frozen for ever in time. These were people who choked to death on the ash. Then the hot ash cooled and set hard round their bodies. Inside, the soft flesh rotted away, leaving only their bones... and a ghostly, body-shaped hollow. In 1860, an Italian archaeologist working at Pompeii had an idea. He removed the bones and filled the hollows with plaster of Paris. When this hardened, it made a plaster cast which could then be dug out of the rock. Giving us a ghastly glimpse of the past.

Historians and archaeologists had a field day finding out what Roman life was really like. Victims of the volcano would no doubt be delighted to know that they didn't die in vain. Here are just a few of the discoveries from Pompeii...

• What the Romans ate and drank – in the remains of taverns, along the streets and in Roman baths they found: eggs, walnuts, figs, (almost) 2,000-year-old bread (a round loaf marked into eight portions was found still in the bread oven in the bakery).

• What the Romans liked to do – they unearthed a two theatres, four temples, a gladiators' barracks and an amphitheatre for gladiator shows.

• What the Romans wore – from mosaics and artefacts they could tell that snake bracelets were all the rage with well-dressed ancient Romans.

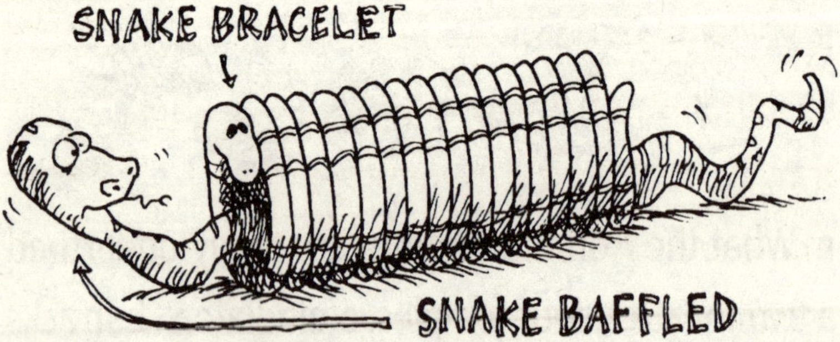

• What pets the Romans kept – one mosaic showed a picture of a guard dog with the words Cave Canem (Beware of the Dog) underneath it; they even found a dog preserved in the ash.

Lethal lahars

Imagine a massive, squelching river of mud, like thick, hot concrete, hurtling at high speed down a volcano's side and you've got a lahar. What's so lethal about lahars is the speed at which they travel – up to 160 kilometres an hour. They're murderous mudflows, formed when water from melting ice mixes with volcanic ash. They bury towns and fields, clog rivers, and shove bridges and buildings out of their way.

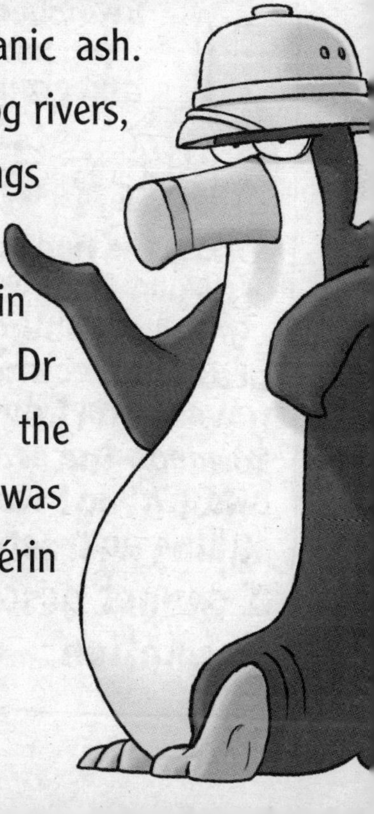

When Mount Pelée erupted in 1902, a rum factory owner, Dr Guérin, witnessed firsthand the havoc a lahar can cause. It was 12.45 pm on 5 May. Dr Guérin was just leaving home…

5 MAY

As I left my house, I heard people shouting, "The mountain's falling down!" Then I heard a noise like nothing on Earth – an immense noise, like the devil. A black avalanche, full of huge blocks, was rolling down the mountain. It left the river bed and rolled against my factory like an army of giant rams. I stood rooted to the spot.

I watched my poor wife and son run towards the shore and prayed for their escape.

Then, all at once, the mud arrived. It passed right in front of me and I felt its deadly breath. There was a great crashing sound and everything was crushed, drowned and submerged. Three black waves swept down, one by one, like thunder towards the sea. My wife and son were swept away. A boat was flung high into the air, killing my trusty foreman.

I cannot describe the desolation.

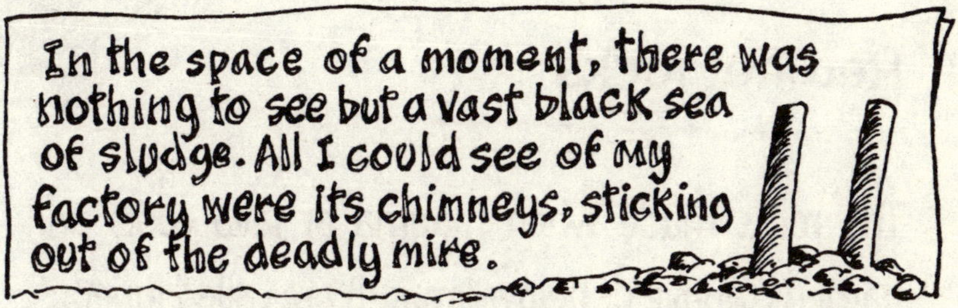

And, by lethal lahar standards, this was quite a low-key affair. When Mount Pinatubo in the Philippines erupted in 1991, the largest lahars ever recorded devastated the surrounding landscape. They left a thousand people dead and 100,000 homeless. Acres of the country's most fertile rice fields were utterly destroyed and several large cities were buried by the mud. The lahars affected than 2.1 million people, with many forced to beg for their living. Even today, the threat isn't over. Vast amounts of ash still cover the mountain and every autumn, when the monsoon rains fall, it turns to mud and starts to flow...

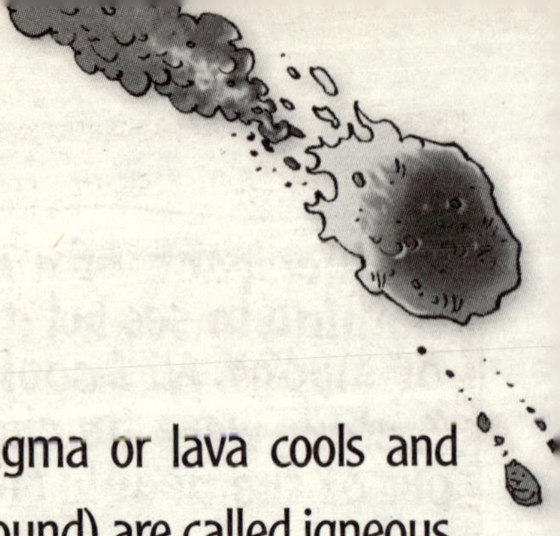

Red-hot rocks

The rocks made when magma or lava cools and hardens (above or below ground) are called igneous, or fire, rocks. There are many different types. But the most famous fire rock, by a long chalk, is...

Looking for that ideal gift? Fed up with giving talc and book tokens? Desperately seeking something different? Then look no further. We have the answer to your prayers. Say goodbye for ever to dull old rubber ducks, with an...

AMAZING... PERPETUAL... PUMICE... BATH DUCK!
A SNIP AT ONLY £59.99*
GUARANTEED SINK PROOF
THE ONLY ROCK THAT FLOATS
OPTIONAL BEADY EYE
MADE FROM BEST OBSIDIAN (BLACK VOLCANIC GLASS)
BEST-QUALITY PUMICE FROM ITALY
(hand-picked by our team of experts)
2 ATTRACTIVE SHADES
WHITE AND GREY
PLEASE STATE WHEN ORDERING
More holes per square cm than cheap imitations
ALSO AVAILABLE *
• Horribly handy-sized pumice stones (for that stubborn hard skin)
• Fabulous floating soap dish (never lose that soap again)
• The latest in armbands (for that nervous swimmer)
WHAT ONE SATISFIED CUSTOMER SAYS...
"My floating soapdish has changed my life"
* WHILE STOCKS LAST

Pumice floats because it's full of hot air. Well, bubbles of gas to be horribly technical. That's why it's full of holes, left when the bubbles go pop. Violent volcanoes blast out millions of tonnes of pimply pumice, from tiny pieces the size of peas to blocks as big as icebergs. Honestly. When Krakatoa erupted in 1883, ships spent months dodging huge hazardous pumice-bergs floating on the sea.

Bright lightning

You often see brilliant flashes of lightning during a violent eruption. This is how they happen.

1 Millions of minuscule fragments

of lava and dust whizz round inside an awesome ash cloud…

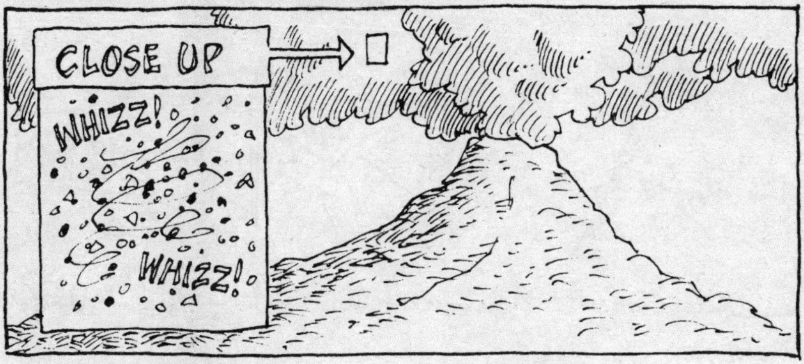

2 … and rub together frighteningly fast.

3 This makes static electricity (the sort you get if you comb your hair very quickly) …

4 ... which shoots out of the cloud as bolts of lightning.

Earth-shattering fact

And now for those fish. Believe it or not, when Mount Tungurahua in Ecuador erupted in 1886, a rain of fish fell on the nearby plains. The fish were thought to have come from a lake in the crater. Apparently, they were none the worse for their strange ordeal, not even slightly battered or lightly fried.

Violent volcanic vocab quiz

Is your geography teacher exploding with volcanic knowledge? Try this quiz on them to find out.

1 What is a'a?

a) the noise you'd make running away from a lava flow

b) a sharp type of rock that cuts easily – best not to touch it with your bare hands

c) a Hawaiian word for lava

2 Where would you find a vug?

a) stopping up a small crater

b) in a volcanologist's rucksack

c) inside a volcanic rock

3 What are lapilli?

a) small bits of rock and lava that blast out of volcanoes

b) small bits of gold found in volcanoes

c) offerings made to volcano gods

4 What would you do with a bread-crust bomb?

a) eat it

b) cook it

c) get out of its way

5 What is pahoehoe?

a) a tool you use to dig through volcanic rock

b) lava in Hawaiian

c) the largest volcano in Hawaii

6 What is a caldera?

a) a circular crater on top of a volcano

b) a circular cone on the side of a volcano

c) a huge pan that old women in pointy black hats are supposed to dance round

7 What is basalt?

a) a volcanic gas

b) a black or grey volcanic rock

c) something you put on your chips

8 What is tuff?

a) a material used to make volcanologists' socks

b) a rock made from volcanic ash

c) a type of grass that can grow on lava

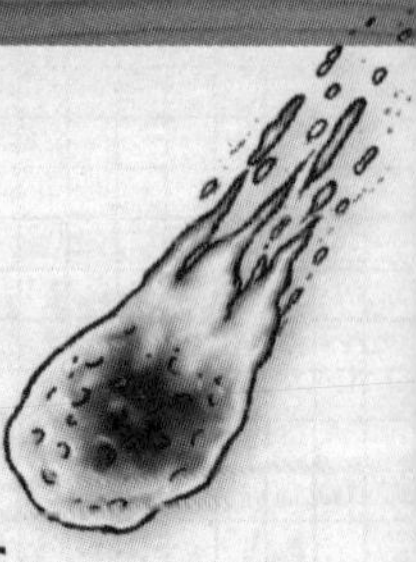

9 What is a fumarole?

a) a type of smoked fish

b) an instrument for measuring fumes

c) a steaming hole in the ground

10 What is a maars?

a) the next planet to Earth

b) a type of volcano

c) a glacier on top of a volcano

ANSWER

1 b) and c) A'a (ah-ah) is thick, sticky lava which forms jagged, chunky rock when it cools. So sharp it can cut the soles off your boots.

2 c) A vug is a hole in a volcanic rock, often lined with crystals. Most vugs are quite small but a cave-sized vug was once discovered. Its crystals filled 1,400 sacks.

3 a) Ranging from pea-sized to apple-sized. Their name means little stones in Latin. Bet your teacher didn't know that!

4 c) A bread-crust bomb is a round blob of lava chucked out of a volcano. It gets its name because as it flies through the air, the outside cools and hardens while the inside stays hot and gooey. This cracks the hard crust, like a loaf of freshly baked bread – but don't try to cook or eat it. Running away is definitely the most sensible option.

5 b) Pahoehoe (pa-hoy-hoy) is runny, fast-flowing lava. Looks like smooth, curly coils of rope when it cools.

6 a) Volcanically speaking, a caldera's a very large crater blasted out when a volcano erupts or when a volcano caves in on itself. But if you want to be clever you could give a mark for c), since 'caldera' is also Spanish for cauldron. Calderas often fill with rainwater to make lofty volcanic lakes. Some are tens of kilometres across.

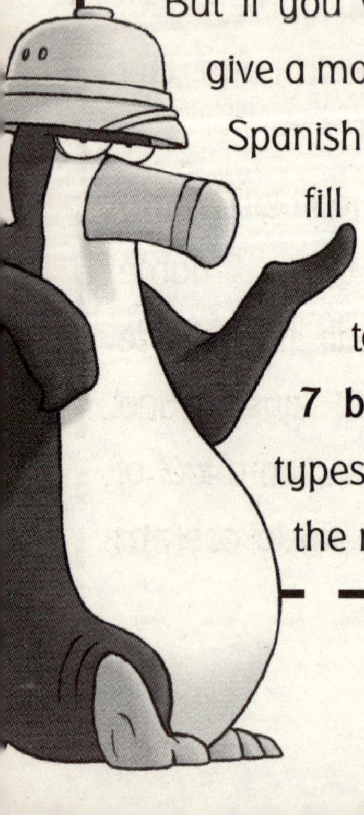

7 b) There are lots of different types of volcanic rocks. Basalt is the most common.

8 b) Very useful for building.

9 c) Found wherever volcanoes are, it spurts steam and smelly gases and is often ringed with crusty yellow sulphur crystals.

10 b) A small volcano formed when magma heats water underground and it explodes to the surface as steam. Absolutely nothing to do with the planet Mars.

What your teacher's score means:

0–4 Oh dear! Sounds like this geography teacher could be nearing 'extinction'.

5–7 Better. Your teacher's no expert but they obviously know their basalt from their table salt.

8–10 Bravo! Your teacher is obviously 'active', and perhaps even a secret volcanologist. Watch out if they start letting off steam.

Of course, apart from being mad, bad and dangerous, volcanoes are fascinating places to visit. So, armed with a smattering of fluent volcano, where on earth should you start your tour?

VIOLENT VOLCANO VISITOR

Tired of all that homework? Looking for a chance to get away? Despite all the hazards, visiting a violent volcano can be horribly exciting. Horribly dangerous? Possibly. Horribly hard to get to? Probably. But don't let any of that put you off. For the first-time traveller, choosing which violent volcano to visit can be extremely tricky. So, to help you plan your trip of a lifetime, *The Daily Globe* is proud to present the following ghastly guide. Enjoy your horribly hot holiday!

THE DAILY GLOBE'S VERY OWN VIOLENT VOLCANO VACATION GUIDE

What's inside:

Hawaiian holidays, sun, sea and sizzlers **(see opposite)**

COMPETITION

WIN THE VOLCANIC VACATION OF A LIFETIME

YOUR CHANCE TO GAWP AT GEYSERS IN THE USA'S YELLOWSTONE PARK

SEE PAGE 65 FOR HOW TO ENTER

Happy hot holiday in Hawaii

Beautiful black sandy beaches

With more than eight million tourists a year, Hawaii's always a hit with the volcano visitor. But what on Earth makes Hawaii so hot? We sent our roving explorer to find out...

I'd always had a hankering to go to Hawaii and now I seized my chance. I wasn't about to be disappointed. The Hawaiian islands are the tops of gigantic volcanoes formed over a hot spot in the Pacific Ocean. Horribly huge but gentle giants. When they erupt, as they often do, they ooze out lava. Oodles and oodles of the sticky stuff, pouring away in great red-hot rivers or filling the air with fireworks. Awesome.

On my second day in Hawaii, I couldn't wait any longer. It was time to go and see an eruption for myself. I went by bus (you can also go by car or helicopter). The fee includes transport, entry into the Hawaii National Park, a snack at

Me in front of bus!

Volcano House cafe and a guided tour. (If you want a T-shirt, it's extra.) For this, you can see the lava bubbling up from the ground and visit a spot where it sizzles into the sea.

With more than 100 islands to choose from, you'll be spoilt

Watch those bubbles - phew!

for choice in hot spot Hawaii. Don't miss Kilauea which has erupted non-stop since 1983. And do make a detour to Mauna Loa, the largest active volcano in the world. Or if you fancy a spot of night viewing, head for the observatory on (dormant) Mauna Kea.

All too soon, it was time to head home. But I'll be back. For the first-time volcano watcher, Hawaii's a must, a horribly exciting chance to see the Earth in action.

PICK OF THE WEEK

Desperate to get away from it all? Try a trip to tiny Tristan da Cunha, the South Atlantic's hidden gem

• Wonder at its wide open spaces – only 400 people in the whole place.

• Bask in blissful peace and quiet – Tristan da Cunha's miles from anywhere. In fact, it's the most isolated island on Earth, about 2,000 kilometres from its nearest neighbours. If you don't believe me, look it up on a map. It's midway between South America and South Africa in the South Atlantic Ocean.

• Gasp at tales of its last eruption in October 1961. It's actually the tip of an underwater volcano that rises 2,062 metres above the sea. And just one in a long chain of undersea volcanoes which snakes right up the Atlantic to Iceland, along a crack where two plates of crust pull apart.

• Enjoy our special offer price – it's excellent value for money. If two of you travel, the third can go free. You'll probably need the company! Call now for a booking form.

THE CASCADE VOLCANOES

YOU KNOW THEY'RE ONLY SLEEPING...

For volcano-watching like never before, visit the Cascade Mountains of north-west USA. Snow-capped peaks, fabulous forests, crystal-clear crater lakes and much, much more. See high-rise Mount Rainier and its 26 glaciers. Marvel at mind-blowing Mount St Helens. Feel the earth shake on hair-raising Mount Hood.

SEND FOR YOUR FREE BROCHURE NOW

Come to the Cascades – they're really cookin'

SKI REPORT

For crisp white snow and stunning scenery, visit Mount Ruapehu (which means "the exploding pit" in Maori) on New Zealand's North Island. The number-one ski spot this year. It's the highest mountain on New Zealand, a towering 2,797 metres tall. Ideal for beginners and experts alike.

HORRIBLE HEALTH WARNING

Expect delays if Mount Ruapehu erupts. Last time it did so, in 2007, ski slopes, roads and nearby airports were forced to close because of falling ash and mud flows. Listen out for news bulletins on radio and TV.

COMPETITION

Your chance to win a week's geyser-watching in fabulous Yellowstone National Park! A geyser is a giant jet of scalding water and steam that's heated to boiling point by hot volcanic rocks sizzling away underground. You'll find them in places like Iceland and New Zealand, too.

But Yellowstone National Park, Wyoming, USA, is home to the most famous, and most enormous, geyser in the world: Steamboat Geyser. This beauty regularly gushes 115 metres high. But don't worry if you miss it – there are another 2,999 geysers in the park to watch out for. Another old favourite, Old Faithful, has let off steam every hour for the last 100 years.

Yellowstone Park sits on one of the Earth's plates above a hot spot. The plate (and Park) slowly drift across the hot spot at a rate of 4.6 cm per year. This is why the rocks underneath it are red hot and that's why those gushing geysers know how to blow.

TO ENTER OUR FABULOUS COMPETITION, FIRST SEE IF YOU CAN ANSWER THESE THREE MIND-BENDING QUESTIONS, THEN COMPLETE THE TIE-BREAK

1: Where is the World's highest geyser?
2: What is it called?
3: Why does a geyser blow?

Complete this sentence in no more than 10 words:

"Steamboat is my kinda geyser because..."

HORRIBLE HOLIDAYS – *taking you close to the edge!*

Meltdown in Fireland

Icelands dotted with deadly volcanoes, making this small island one of the shakiest places on Earth. More Fireland than Iceland, with an eruption every five years – it's a must for every volcano watcher. Iceland's scientists thought they'd seen it all. Until, that is, the dramatic events of autumn 1996, when something sinister seemed to be stirring beneath the ice...

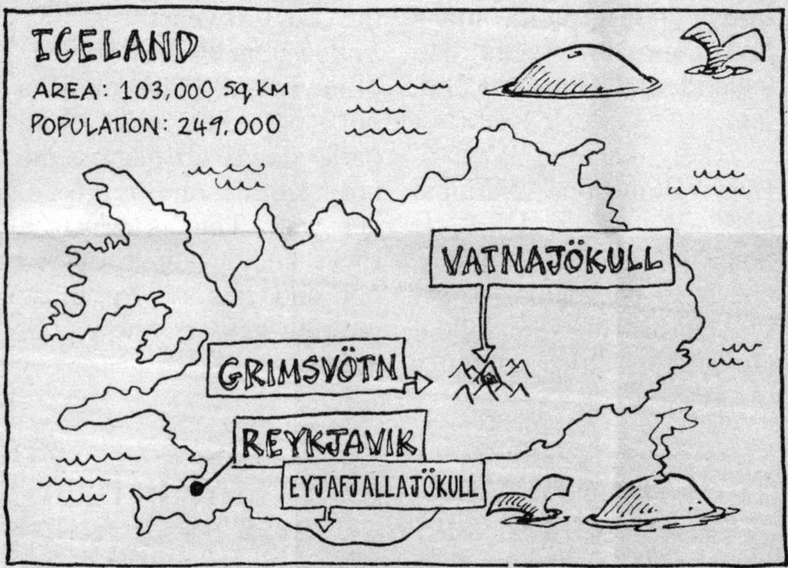

For six long weeks, scientists had been monitoring the ghastly Grimsvötn volcano, flying back and forth in an observer plane. The warning signs were already there, with a tell-tale series of earthquakes showing magma stirring deep underground. It seemed the volcano was getting ready to blow. But that wasn't all. Above the volcano lay Vatnajökull, the largest glacier in Europe, covering one-tenth of the island. If the heat of the volcano melted the ice, it could trigger off the most terrible floods Iceland had ever known. The anxious, scientists held their breath, and watched...

Then, one day, their worst fears were realized. Cracks appeared in the smooth, icy face of the glacier – the earth-shattering eruption had begun. Beneath the ice, the volcano was boiling, melting an incredible 6,000 tonnes of ice every second. By day three of the eruption, its awesome energy had blasted through 760 metres of ice and melted a vast, yawning chasm in the ice, 3 kilometres wide, which belched out black clouds of steam and ash.

The scientists were baffled. They had seen the ice melt with their own eyes but where on Earth had all the water gone? The emergency teams braced themselves for the onslaught, working round the clock to put up barriers to halt the huge flow of water. Parts of the south coast were closed to traffic. Suddenly, almost three weeks later, they got their answer. As if a huge dam had burst, the dreaded flood came. Three thousand billion tonnes of water poured out of the glacier, at a startling speed of 55,000 cubic metres a second.

It tore icebergs the size of houses from the glacier, and

swept away roads, bridges, power stations and electricity lines. Eventually, it sped out to sea, leaving fields of icebergs stranded on the shore. The worst was over. When the scientists came to survey the damage, the full force of the massive flood became clear. It was Iceland's worst flood for 60 years, but the Icelanders were lucky! Vatnajökull lies in the empty south of Iceland. The few hundred people who lived near by had already been evacuated. Though millions of pounds of damage were caused, incredibly, no human lives were lost.

Iceland is one of the most horribly shaky places on Earth. This is because it lies astride two plates of the Earth's crust, one carrying North America and the other, Europe and Asia. Slowly but surely, the plates are moving apart, by 4 cm every year. Luckily for the islanders, volcanic eruptions form new land in between to plug the gap.

BOOK OF THE WEEK

KRAKATOA: THERE SHE BLOWS

by Captain E. Ruption

Based on an eyewitness account, *Krakatoa: There She Blows* tells the story of the most violent volcanic eruption ever. On 27 August 1883, after slumbering quietly for 200 years, Krakatoa, a volcanic island in south-west Indonesia, suddenly exploded. Ash and pumice blasted 50 kilometres into the air. Two-thirds of the island slumped into the sea. The captain of a passing cargo ship watched Krakatoa blow. He noted in his log:

"The deafening explosions sounded like gunfire while lumps of gas-charged lava exploded in the sky, like a gigantic firework display. Just after 5 pm the ship's decks were bombarded with hot pumice; some pieces were as large as pumpkins. Ash fell so rapidly on the decks that the crew worked non-stop to keep them clear."

Miraculously, the captain and crew survived. Others weren't so lucky. The explosion triggered a huge tsunami, or tidal wave, which raced towards the low-lying coasts of Java and Sumatra. 163 villages were swept away. A staggering 36,000 people died.

In this gripping book, Captain E. Ruption paints a vivid picture of that dreadful day. Ideal reading for your horrible holiday. (Unless you're off to Indonesia, perhaps. You don't want to push your luck.)

Highly recommended.

LATE BREAKS

Cotopaxi
(cot-oh-pak-see), Ecuador
Adventure awaits you in the Andes.
Must be fit – Cotopaxi is 5,897 metres high. If you're feeling lazy, you can go halfway up by car, then cycle down! Honestly! Phase: Active.

Popocatepetl
(pop-oh-cat-a-pet-ul), Mexico
But you can call it Popo, for short. This snow-capped peak is 5,426 metres high and last erupted in 2015. Local legend says Popo was a giant whom the gods turned to stone. Try nearby Mexico City for places to stay. Phase: Active.

Etna, Sicily, Italy
Europe's largest active volcano, Mount Etna is 3,330 metres tall. You can get to the top by bus or car. If you decide to walk, you'll be in good company – one of the first people to climb Mount Etna was the hardy Roman emperor, Hadrian. Last major eruption 1991–1993. Small eruption at the beginning of 1998, so take a hard hat. Phase: Active.

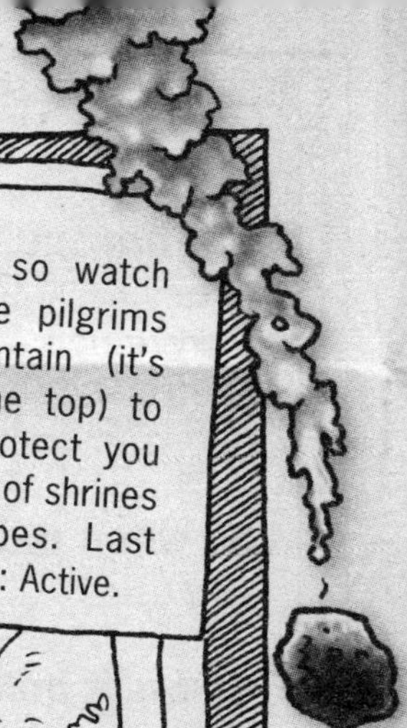

Fuji, Japan
A sacred volcano, so watch your step. Join the pilgrims climbing the mountain (it's 3,776 metres to the top) to ask the gods to protect you from harm. Hundreds of shrines to visit on the slopes. Last eruption 1707. Phase: Active.

Kilimanjaro, Tanzania
The highest mountain in Africa (at a towering 5,895 metres). Two peaks – Kibo and Mawenzi, joined by a ridge. Snap the ice cap on Kibo's crater. Coffee grows on the volcano's slopes. Phase: Extinct/Dormant.

QUICK GUIDE Mount Erebus

Mount Erebus, where on earth is that?
On the east coast of Ross Island, in icy Antarctica, actually.

They can't have volcanoes there, it's far too cold!
That's where you're wrong – they most certainly do. There's another one called Mount Terror, but that's not as bad as it sounds: it's extinct. Mount Erebus is very much alive.

All right, I believe you. So how high is this freaky peak?
About 3,794 metres, at the last count.

Hmmm, quite a size. And does it still breathe fire?
Very much so. Beneath its icy exterior, it's red hot and raring to go – you can tell by the steam pouring out of its top.

So when did it last erupt?
1989.

And is it horribly violent?
Well, it can be, but it doesn't get many visitors, so no one's usually around to see it.

Phew, so no danger to humans then?
Well, it has had its moments. In 1979, a plane carrying sightseers from New Zealand crashed into Mount Erebus, killing everyone on board.

Sounds violent to me. What's so special about it?
Well, in the main crater there's a big lake … filled with bubbling lava.

Wow, now you're talking. But if nobody goes there, how do we know it's there?
A Scottish explorer, Sir James Ross, found it in 1841.

Lucky Sir James. What was he doing there?
Exploring, you idiot. That's what explorers usually do.

And did he call it Erebus?
Yes, after one of his ships. It's another word for Hell.

I'd say that was a pretty appropriate name!

AUNTIE VI'S TOP TEN TRAVELLERS' TIPS

but you know how much your Auntie Vi worries about you. So, I've put together a few essential tips to make your journey safer. I simply *won't* let you go if you're not prepared!

1 If the volcano you're visiting is active, do BE CAREFUL, loveys – it could quickly turn nasty. Always consult the experts first, will you do that for me? They'll show you a nice safe place to watch from.

2 Now, I know it's hot up those volcanoes, but you must promise to wrap up. You'll need several extra layers of clothes to put on – a nice thick thermal vest would be ideal, dears. Yes, it might start off warm at the foot of a volcano but, mark my words, it can get ever so nippy at the top.

3 You must watch out for those moving lava flows, and whatever you do, DON'T WALK OVER ONE! Well, they sometimes look rock solid on top, but believe me, underneath, the rocks'll be bubbling more fierily than one of my pepperoni hot pots. You could really put your foot in it.

4 Thick-soled boots are a must, loveys. Yes, even in summer. Volcanic rock can be sharp as razors; it'd slice right through those flimsy trainer things you wear so much.

5 Geysers and hot springs. Now, they're lovely to look at, aren't they, luvies, but always, always, STICK TO THE PATHS. You never know when a thin crust of rock might be hiding a pool of scorching water. Put one foot wrong and you'll be boiled alive. Then you'll be sorry you didn't listen to your Auntie Vi!

6 If you're near a volcano that's even thinking about producing a pyroclastic flow, GET OUT FAST! It will *always* win, loveys.

7 Now if you make it safely to the crater, watch out for volcanic domes that can grow inside. Sometimes they'll just suddenly explode without warning, darlings! Never *ever* go near one that's less than ten years old.

8 It might sound obvious, but I'll mention this one just in case – don't camp near streams running from volcanoes. You wouldn't really want to be swept away by a flood or lava now, would you, loveys?

9 And you'd best avoid craters that are full of gas, too. Those volcanic gases

can be horribly poisonous. You might not be able to hold your breath for long enough to get away. Oh, dear, I can't bear to think of it.

10 Finally, if you must go, always treat volcanoes, violent or otherwise, with respect, loveys. After all, you can never tell what they're up to. Oh, and don't forget to send a postcard to your Auntie Vi, will you? You know how anxious I get.

WEATHER WATCH

When choosing your volcanic vacation, don't forget that volcanoes can seriously damage the weather.

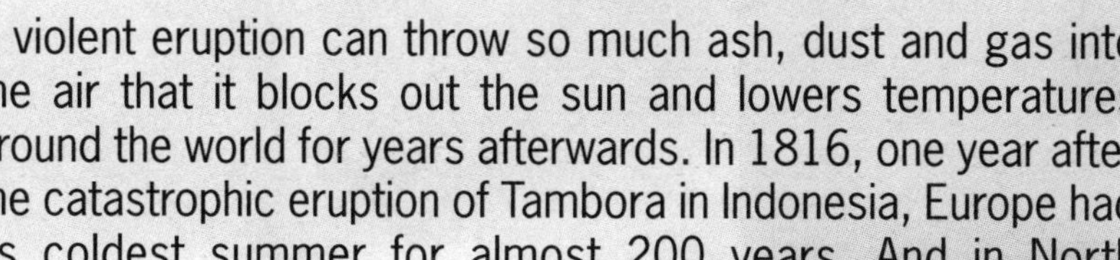

A violent eruption can throw so much ash, dust and gas into the air that it blocks out the sun and lowers temperatures around the world for years afterwards. In 1816, one year after the catastrophic eruption of Tambora in Indonesia, Europe had its coldest summer for almost 200 years. And in North America temperatures fell by 6°C. The wintry weather killed off crops and caused widespread hunger, death and disease, becoming known as "the year without summer".

Going on holiday is one thing. But would you want to live on a live volcano? You might be surprised. There are plenty of people who do just that.

HORRIBLE HIGH LIFE

Fancy having a volcano for your next-door neighbour? No? Well, millions of people can't be wrong. Or can they? Around 500 million people currently live near an active volcano. Why do they do it? Is it worth the risk? What happens if the volcano turns nasty? Is there anything in it for them? Let's have a look at the pros and cons.

Killer mountains?

First, the cons. However you look at it, having your home next to a volcano can be horribly hazardous...

- In the 20th century alone, about 90,000 people were killed in eruptions.
- Lethal lava can burn and bulldoze everything in its path.
- Choking ash and mud can smother the countryside, devastating farmers' fields and crops, cutting off communications and bringing transport to a halt. In a violent eruption, you stand to lose your home, your livelihood ... and your life. Overnight, a volcano can turn your world into a wasteland. It can take a region hundreds of years to recover. If it ever does.

• There can be sinister side-effects on the world's weather, too, like tsunamis (remember Krakatoa?), starvation and disease. And it can cost millions and millions of pounds to clean up the mess.

And then there's the awful uncertainty. Violent volcanoes are horribly unpredictable. One minute, you're happily living in paradise. The next, your world's been turned upside down. As the people of Montserrat, a tiny, beautiful tropical island in the sunny Caribbean, found to their cost in July 1995, when Chance's Peak, a dormant volcano in the south of the island, suddenly woke up...

TROUBLE IN PARADISE

ROSE'S DIARY

KEEP OUT!

18 JULY 1995

Dear Diary

Strange things are happening in my town. On our way back from school today, we were playing I-spy. My Sister spotted something beginning BS. After what seemed like ages, I gave up, and she said, "Black snow, you idiot!" She is only eight and she's got a wild imagination! So I played along with her, but then

My sister

I saw what she meant. It looked like smoke was coming from the Soufriere Hills behind the town – they're more like mountains really – and big specks of ash were starting to fall from

the sky. It really did look like black snow. It doesn't usually snow at all on Montserrat, so I started to feel really spooked.

After tea we raced over to grandma's. She knows everything there is to know, so we asked her why the mountain was smoking.

Grandma

"Oh, you don't need to worry about that, girls," she said "The scientists will sort it out. That's what they're paid for. That old volcano's been fast asleep for 400 years and it's not about to wake up now."

Still I couldn't remember seeing anything like the smoke and the snow before, and I have been around for a whole ten years.

20 July 1995

We haven't been to school for two days now. So it has to be serious. The volcano is starting to erupt. First it started to rumble, then huge rocks and stones started shooting out of the top. Like this.

Even in the middle of the day, it got really dark. Mr Dyer, our next door neighbour, was dead nervous - I've never seen him like that before. He's got some fields on the mountain side where he grows sweet potatoes and carrots and keeps his goats. He can't go and visit them now, though, it's far too risky. I wonder what the goats must be thinking? My Mum tried her best to calm him down but she didn't sound convincing - her voice went all wobbly and that's usually bad news.

26 July 1995

Things are getting worse and worse. Our house is now covered in thick, black ash - and half the town is too - it's horrible. I daren't breathe too deeply in case I swallow some of it. When we turned on the TV, a man was saying that the volcano could erupt at any time now...
What's going to happen to us all?

26 August 1995

The volcano was still huffing and blowing and things got really bad. In the end, the government said it was too dangerous for people to carry on living in Plymouth – that's the capital of Montserrat, and where I live!

My home town was dangerous! That took a bit of getting used to. It was just too close to the volcano. We all had to move to the north of the island where it was safer. My dad closed up our shop and locked up the house and we packed our things and were off. Grandma came too. (She's not very happy with that volcano – she's even more annoyed with the scientists, though!) In fact the whole town was on the move.

You should have seen the chaos, cars were piled high with boxes and suit-cases, and blankets and bedding. We couldn't even say goodbye to Mr Dyer's goats. And there was no way he could take them with him. Then there really would be chaos. We've been here for about a month now. All our friends are here too so it's just like home – except we haven't got a home of course. We sleep in the church and go to school in a tent! Believe it or not, Dad's got into dominoes in a big way, and every night there's the domino challenge.

14 March 1997

We're still in the camp - it's like a little town now with its own shop which Dad runs and a hospital. We moved out of the church into a wooden house. It's quite nice but a bit squashed. Everyone's squashed here, though. Some people who live in huge houses have to share their luxury bedrooms. Some people even got to stay in tourist hotels and holiday homes - my Dad says they still have to pay, even though it isn't much of a holiday.

Last night there was a gospel concert in one of the hotels. It was great, just like church used to be on Sundays: I really thought the roof might lift off! They made such a beautiful sound.

It's funny how people can be so cheerful when everything seems to be going wrong. Grandma says people are just, "putting a brave face on things" and deep down we're all a bit fed up. My Mum says, "you have to laugh, or else you cry."

The volcano is STILL erupting. poor Mr Dyer's fields have all gone. They've been buried in ash and rock. Now he doesn't know what he'll do. (I'm trying not to think about the goats.) And lot's of people have got bad coughs from breathing in all the ash. I've stopped asking when we can go home - I think it was getting on mum's nerves. And we might not be able to - ever! It all depends on the volcano. And no one knows what it'll do!

21 march 1997

I had a dream last night that everything was OK We were living back home and everything was normal. The mango tree in the garden was bursting with fresh, juicy fruit. I was at my old school and all my old friends were there as if nothing had happened. The sky was a deep blue, the hill sides were rich green and dotted with orange and yellow flowers, just like they used to be. I felt great when I woke up, but then I remembered where I was, and what one man said yesterday – "Everything back home is grey. It looks like you've walked into a black and white photograph." – and I knew we would never go back.

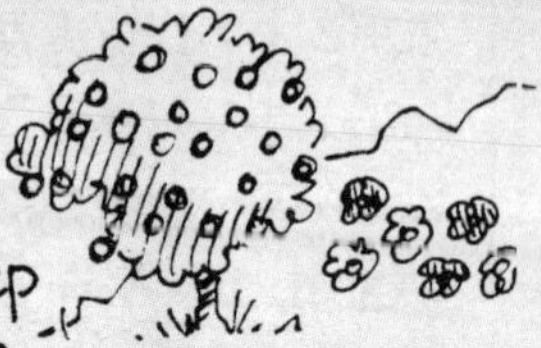

21 July 1997 – London, England

Such a lot has happened in the last few months that I haven't had time to write. One day, my Dad came home from the shop and told us he'd made a decision. We were leaving Montserrat and going to England to live. Lots of people had already gone and others had gone to Antigua. Next thing I knew we were on a boat sent from England and off on our journey across the world. Me and my sister cried and cried as the boat pulled out of the harbour.

Montserrat looked beautiful as we left, but when we got further away, we could see smoke and I knew we had to go. Grandma decided to stay behind. She said she was much too old to start travelling now. And anyway, the volcano might go quiet again. It hasn't yet! It's still erupting and there could be a really big explosion any day now.

It's OK living with my Uncle in London and going to a new school but all I want is to go home. It's so cold here! And I miss so many things. These are just a few of them:

- The steaming heat that cools down when the rain comes.
- Squidging black sand through my toes on the beaches (we used to walk to the beach from our house). It's because of the volcano that the sand's black.
- The tropical turquoise sea and catching fish with my dad.
- Friday night street parties (I used to watch them from my bedroom window).
- Dressing up for church on Sunday.

Goatwater stew and Grandma's sugar cake - made from fresh coconut, yum.

But most of all, I miss my Grandma.

I suppose I'll get used to living here, but I can't help my dreams about being at home, and I can't help feeling disappointed when I wake up. Rosie age 12½

Big, friendly giants?

Given the danger, why on earth would anyone choose to live near an active volcano? You might be surprised.

Magma, Lava & Ash, Estate Agents

One house, slightly ashy. Great views over the valley. Steeply sloping, terraced garden. With built-in volcano-proof bunker. Some subsidence likely.

Some red-hot reasons for living near a volcano

1 Fabulously fertile soil. Volcanic soil is the richest on Earth. Especially after a light dusting of ash. And chock-full of nourishment to help plants prosper. From ancient times, volcanoes have been heavily farmed and today provide food for millions of people.

Some of the best rice-growing land in Indonesia, for example, lies in the shadow of active volcanoes. It's so

fantastically fertile, farmers can grow three crops, not one, every year. Since the days of Pompeii, fine wines have come from volcanic vineyards on the slopes of Mount Vesuvius. Not to mention coffee from the craters of Central America. Of course, you can have too much of a good thing. If the ash is too thick, about 20 centimetres or more, it kills fields dead.

2 Cheap central heating. In volcanic regions, underground water gets superheated to 150°C. This can be pumped directly into people's homes for washing and central heating. Or it can be converted into cheap electricity. It's called geothermal energy and it's cheap, clean and won't run out. No wonder geographers love it! It means that in places like icy Iceland, you can take a midwinter dip in a heated swimming-pool.

Outdoors! Or eat tropical fruit like bananas and pineapples which are grown in geothermal greenhouses.

3 Loads of lava. Lava is horribly useful. How? For a start, you can…

- live in it. Since the 4th century CE, people in Cappadocia, Turkey, have hollowed out cave-like homes, and even churches, inside lava cones. It's easy to dig, strong, fireproof and an excellent insulator (keeps you warm in winter and cool in summer) to boot. What more could you possibly ask for?

• stone-wash your jeans with it. You know those faded jeans your dad still wears that used to be trendy? Well, the stone they're washed with is … pumice!

• house-train your cat in it. Lots of cat litter is actually volcanic ash. Great for soaking up those things cats do.

• improve your looks with it. (Well, the looks of your feet anyway.) If hard skin's a problem, get straight to work with a pumice stone. They've been used for centuries. In fact, baffled archaeologists at work on a dig thought the place had been pummelled by pumice during a volcanic eruption. Except that there wasn't a volcano near by. Then, they realized that people had probably been pummelling themselves with pumice stones for centuries to smooth their skin – they'd bought the stones from Roman traders who were a very long way from home.

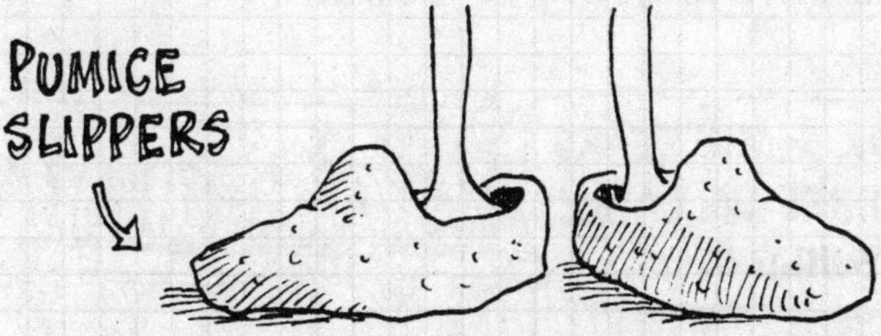

LOSE THAT HARD SKIN AS YOU WALK

4 Brilliant building blocks. Rock made from volcanic ash is tuff by name and tough by nature. Cut into blocks, it's brilliant for building. Houses, roads, bridges, you name it. And concrete. It was the Romans who invented concrete and completely changed building techniques, by building structures that actually stayed standing. And the secret ingredient in concrete? Volcanic dust, as if you hadn't guessed! Without volcanoes, you wouldn't have had such staggering structures as the Colosseum, or the Pantheon or Roman roads that your history teacher is always going on about.

5 Marvellous metals. What do copper, lead, tin, silver and gold have in common? The answer is they're all found in magma. Mining these metals is big business. Though it's best to wait for the volcano to cool. You can also find gold in volcanic hot springs.

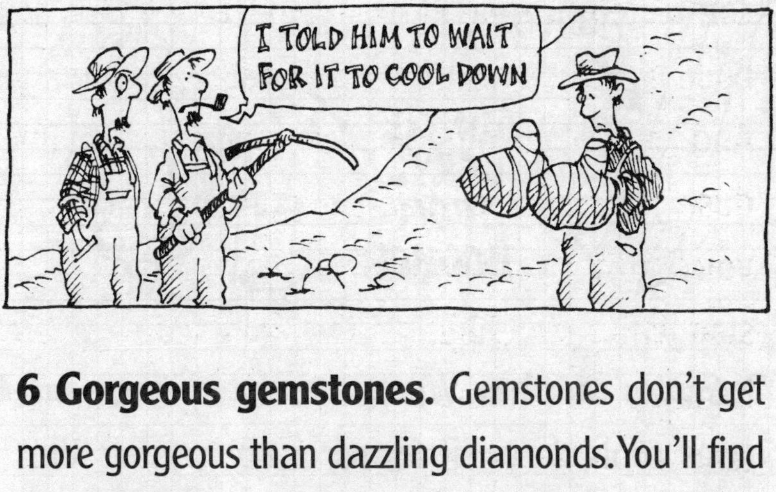

6 Gorgeous gemstones. Gemstones don't get more gorgeous than dazzling diamonds. You'll find these sparklers in volcanic rock (called kimberlite). If you're lucky. And if the volcano's been extinct for at least a couple of million years. Diamonds are formed deep inside the Earth and churned up by volcanoes, especially in South Africa and Western Australia. Even more precious is rare red beryl from Utah in the USA. Chip out one little beryl and you could be seriously rich!

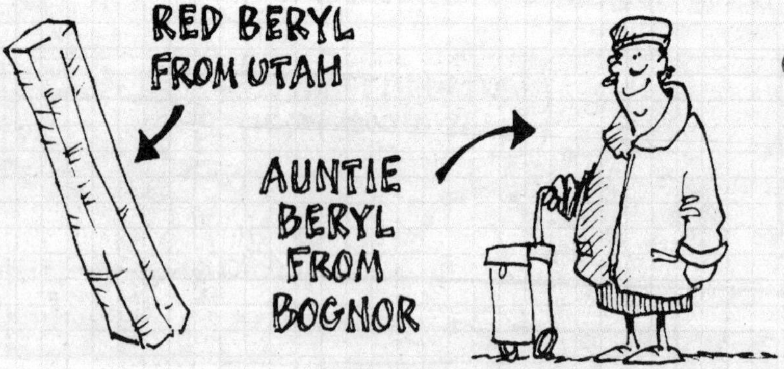

7. Super sulphur. When the sulphur in volcanic gases cools down, it forms crusty crystals that are a brilliant yellow colour. You see them around hot springs and fumaroles. Sulphur is mined in Italy, Chile and Japan. It's used to make matches, gunpowder, dyes and ointments (and it stinks!

It's the same stuff that's used to make stink bombs). It's also added to rubber to make it tougher for tyres. This process is called vulcanization, after good old Vulcan.

Earth-shattering fact

If all else fails, why not save on electricity and use your volcano as an oven? That's what villagers on Mount Unzen, Japan do. Forget about egg-timers and boiling water! They use the hot steam gushing out of the volcano to hard-boil eggs for lunch.

Horrible Health Warning

If you're thinking of risking life on the lava, it pays to be careful. Very careful. So, how can you tell if a violent volcano is about to erupt? Here are some warning signs to listen and look out for.

Other telltale signs include…

• Barking: it's said that dogs get restless before an eruption!

• Smelly fumes: levels of toxic gases rise with the magma. Very dangerous. By the time these gases get up your nose, it could be too late. Some are smellier than others, e.g. stinky sulphur dioxide which smells like rotten eggs. Some are acids which can bleach or eat your clothes (and skin). But the deadliest of all, carbon dioxide, has no odour. Which makes it horribly hard to detect.

The terrible (true) tale of the killer lake

Night had fallen on 21 August 1986. In the village of Lower Nyos, Cameroon, most people were already fast asleep and did not hear the sound of a small explosion at nearby Lake Nyos. Those who heard it thought nothing of it. Little did they realize the terrible danger they were in.

The noise signalled the release from the lake of a huge cloud of poisonous gases, 50 metres thick. The deadly fumes poured silently down the valley, suffocating 1,700 people. In Lower Nyos alone, 1,200 people died. The handful of survivors told how they had seen people simply drop down dead in the middle of eating or talking. The morning brought another grisly scene – the fields around Lower Nyos were strewn with the bodies of thousands of cattle. For 21 August had been market day. Unusually, no flies or vultures hovered around the bodies. They too had been caught in the killer cloud's path.

The gases came from Lake Nyos, a small, deep lake which had formed inside a volcanic crater. Over hundreds of years, toxic gases leaking from the volcano had collected in the water at the bottom of the lake. The main gas was deadly poisonous carbon dioxide, undetectable because it has no smell. On that fateful August night, something happened in the lake to trigger the release of the gases. Heavy rains or a small earthquake may have stirred up the water, bringing the gases to the surface. But no one knows for certain. Whatever the reasons for the killer cloud, the results were catastrophic. It suffocated every living thing in its path until it was scattered by the wind and rain. Thousands of people fled their homes, too terrified to live by the lake a moment longer.

Sadly, warning signs aren't always reliable. No two volcanoes behave the same. A violent eruption may be minutes, months, or even years away. And there are often false alarms – you never can be certain. Sometimes you get no warning at all, even if you do know what to watch out for...

STAYING ALIVE

If a violent volcano blows its top, there's not a lot you can do. Except get out of its way. Fast!

If you pick a fight with a volcano, the volcano will always win. Well, almost always. A few brave souls have taken on volcanoes and won. Others have tried ... but failed. Others are still trying. Very trying.

The Daily Globe

12 May 1902, Martinique, West Indies

PRISONER IN ERUPTION ESCAPE SHOCK

In the aftermath of last week's devastating eruption, a shocked prisoner is today celebrating a miraculous escape from death. In an interview with this paper, the man, Louis-Auguste Ciparis, told our reporter, "I must be the luckiest man alive."

PRISONER SET FREE

Very lucky indeed. Condemned to die at dawn on 9 May, Ciparis was spending his final days in a dungeon-like cell under St Pierre jail. Lucky because, in the once-bustling town of St Pierre, he was one of only two people left alive.

Meanwhile, the island is struggling to come to terms with the terrible tragedy. Mount Pelée, dormant for centuries, had shown signs of stirring for several weeks. In mid-April, a sugar refinery high on the slopes was destroyed in a minor eruption. On 25 April a shower of ash fell like ghostly snow on St Pierre, turning day to night. But the authorities still said there was nothing to fear. Then, at 7.45 a.m., on 8 May, the sleeping volcano began to wake up. The whole shattering event was witnessed by Fernand Clerc, a wealthy farmer from St Pierre. On a hunch, he and his family had packed up and left town. They were the only ones to do so. From a safe distance, they watched in horror as the whole south side of the mountain suddenly blew apart, blasting out a huge rolling black cloud.

MT PELEE BLOWS ITS TOP

"It was like a thousand enormous cannon," Mr Clerc told us. "Firing out scorching steam and rocks."

He went on to describe to me how, before their terrified eyes, this hellish cloud of ash, rock and fire (known technically as a pyroclastic flow) hurtled down the mountainside at incredible speed, "like a red-hot hurricane of fire". It swallowed up everything in its path.

In seconds, it reached St Pierre. There was no way of escape. Some people were suffocated. Others were buried. Others were burned to death. All but three of the town's 30,000 inhabitants perished (apart from Ciparis, another man and a ten-year-old girl survived).Then the deadly cloud flowed into the sea where it made the water hiss and boil. In the harbour, ships were torn from their moorings and flung out to sea. For seven terrible hours the nightmare continued.

ST PIERRE IN RUINS

Then Mount Pelée at last grew quiet once more.

Among the burned-out ruins of St Pierre, Louis-Auguste Ciparis was found four days later, in his cell, still calling weakly for help. Perhaps the only one for whom the volcano brought good fortune, he has since been granted his freedom – both his accusers and would-be executioners are now dead.

Earth-shattering fact

Fer de lance snakes are some of the most vicious vipers in the world. They usually live in the rainforests of South and Central America. The fer de lance will only sink its enormous fangs into human flesh if it's disturbed – but when it does bite, the victim dies. (It's incredible, then, that some local people used to catch the snakes and fire them at their enemies, using a special blow-pipe.) When Mount Pelee erupted, 50 people were killed by deadly fer de lance snakes which had been disturbed by all the mess and din.

Saved by the cell

The violent eruption of Mount Pelée ranks as one of the 20th century's worst volcanic disasters. As for Louis-Auguste Ciparis? He later became a bit of a celebrity, touring the world as a circus act. (He called himself Ludger Sylbaris. For some reason!) He owed his life to the thick stone walls of his cell. Many years later, this gave scientists a good idea... Using Ciparis's cell as a model, they designed a new type of volcano shelter. To make your own, here's what to do.

What you need:

- a large concrete pipe about 2 metres wide
- a hillside (volcanic)

What you do:

1 Bury the pipe in the hillside like this:

2 Add a door at the end.

3 Stock up on tinned food, bedding, books, gas masks, tin opener etc.

4 At the first sign of an eruption, take cover. Simple! But even when you think you're in the perfect position to avoid a volcano, you may not be as safe as you think. You might think that a jet plane would be the perfect place to be, but you'd be wrong…

Almost a mid-air dis-ash-ter

"Good evening, ladies and gentlemen, this is your captain, Eric Moody, speaking. We hope you enjoyed your evening meal. You might be interested to know that, although it's dark outside, if you look through your window, the lights you can see below are on the island of Sumatra, Indonesia. We're now heading towards Java, cruising at a height of 11,500 metres.

We're set for a comfortable few hours' journey, so sit back and enjoy the in-flight movie."

Everything seemed perfectly normal.

It was 24 June, 1982. British Airways Flight 9, a Boeing 747-200, was en route from Malaysia to Perth, Australia, with 247 passengers and 16 crew on board. And they were all in for a terrible shock.

Captain Moody had just left his seat to talk to the passengers, when his co-pilot called him back to the flight deck. Through the cockpit window, they could see a dazzling display of lightning, like an incredible fireworks display. A breathtaking sight, they agreed.

Then came a series of extraordinary events. First, the number four engine failed – this wasn't especially unusual, and as there were another three engines, the crew weren't especially worried. But then, inexplicably, one after the other, the other three engines failed. In the space of a minute, all four engines had stopped running. The impossible had happened.

Quickly, the captain sent out a mayday call.

"Jakarta, Jakarta. Mayday! Mayday! This is Speedbird 9. We have lost all engines. Repeat, we have lost all engines!"

The first the passengers knew of the danger that faced them was when the beam from the movie projector seemed to fill up with smoke with no sign of a fire. Captain Moody made a short announcement: "Ladies and gentlemen, we have a small problem. We've lost all four engines. We're doing our damnedest to get them going again. We hope you're not in too much distress."

Gradually, the smoke got thicker until the oxygen masks came down. Then all the lights went out in the cabin. Over the next few minutes, the plane plunged thousands of metres through the air as the crew tried in vain to restart the engines.

The terrified passengers sat in pitch darkness and in silence – except for the eerie creaking of the fuselage. For, with no power, there was no air conditioning and no noise. They felt sure they were going to die.

For 16 heart-stopping minutes, the plane fell. It seemed an eternity, but then, at about 4,000 metres, one of the engines suddenly restarted. Closely followed by another. And, at the last minute, the third and fourth engines started with a mighty roar. It wasn't only the engines that roared. Their was a roar from the passengers too; some had tears streaming down their faces. Their relief was overwhelming.

The crew prepared for an emergency landing at Jakarta airport. Despite poor visibility – the windscreen had been badly sandblasted – the plane landed smoothly, and safely. Thanks to the expertise of the pilots, the badly shocked passengers had a lucky escape.

What Captain Moody didn't know was that the cause of the shut-down was a huge ash cloud, from the eruption of the Galunggung volcano on Java. The plane had flown right through it, sucking choking ash into its engines. The awful ash clogged the engines, causing them to stall.

As the plane fell, the engines restarted because rushing air blew the ash away. But why hadn't the crew spotted the cloud? For a start, it was night, so they couldn't see it, and it didn't show up on the radar screen. And, although Galunggung had been belching out ash for several months now, no one had thought to warn them…

There's no need to panic! Things have got better since then. Pilots are now trained to spot warning signs, such as lightning and a strong pong like rotten eggs. Then, instead of **1** speeding up (to shake the ash out of the engines) or **2** flying up and out of the cloud, they are told to **1** slow down (to lower the temperature inside the engines so the glassy ash doesn't melt and clog them up), **2** turn around and fly back out of the cloud, or **3** not take off at all. In 2010, planes around the world were grounded when a volcano called Eyjafjallajokull erupted ashily in Iceland.

Meanwhile, back on the ground…

Stopping the flow

Picture the scene… The lava's flowing straight towards you, your home is under threat, all your precious gadgets, and your priceless stamp collection, are about to go up in smoke. You've got to act fast. But what can you do? Is it ever possible to stop the flow? Or even divert it out of harm's way? Here are a few tried and tested methods, but do they work? Decide which method you think works best, then check out the answers on pages 101–3.

1 Build a dam across it. There have been many attempts at diverting lava flows by blocking their path with a wall or barrier. The idea is the lava piles up higher and higher on one side of the wall, then dribbles gently over the top.

2 Take a shovel to it. On Mount Etna, in 1669, workers attacked a lava flow with picks and shovels to try to push it away from their town.

3 Bomb it. Sometimes the top of lava goes cool and crusty while it's still hotly flowing below. So pick your moment, then drop the bomb. The idea is that the bomb breaks the crust and slows down the flow by clogging it up with solid lava chunks. Which makes the lava spill out sideways and weakens the force of the flow. You hope!

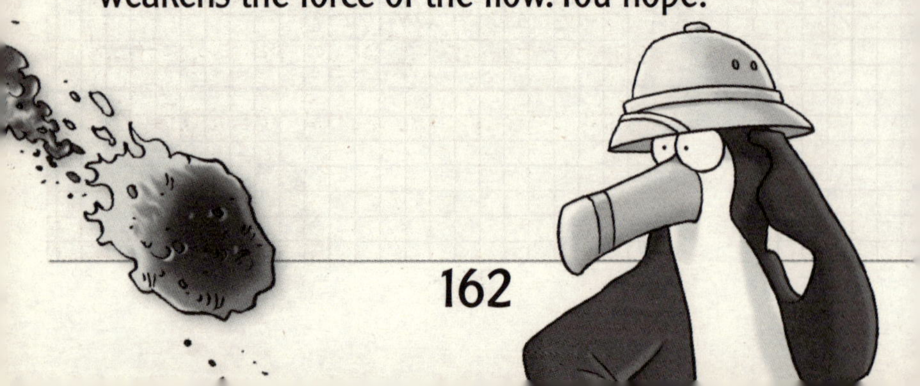

4 Hose it down. Use cold water hose and spray it in the direction of the lava to make it set rock hard. That should stop it in its tracks or at least make it change its course.

In January 1973, the islanders of Heimaey in Iceland watched in horror as a huge crack, 2 kilometres long, opened up on the edge of the main town of Vestmannaeyjar. Within days, the boiling earth below had built a volcano more than 200 metres high where a tranquil meadow had once been. Thick black ash rained down on the town. Wherever you looked, fires raged. But more omnious still was the huge river of lava creeping slowly but surely towards the harbour. Without the harbour, there would be no fishing industry ... and no Heimaey. Most of the islanders left for safety but one group of men stayed behind, determined to fight back. What on earth could they do to lure the lava away? The days passed by. Then the weeks. Time was fast running out. Then someone had an idea. They organized a system of fire engines and set to work hosing the lava down with millions of litres of sea water. But would it work?

5 Divert it. When Etna erupted, between 1991 and 1993, valiant volcanologists built a new channel next to the lava flow. Then they used explosives to block the path of the lava. The idea was that the explosives would divert the lava into their home-made channel.

6 Offer it a sacrifice. If all else fails, you could always try a short prayer or a sacrifice. That's what people in Hawaii have done for years. They believe that Kilauea is the home of the fiery goddess, Pele, who lives inside the volcano's crater. You can see her breath in the steam. When she's angry, she stamps her feet and makes the volcano erupt. (She's clearly got a terrible temper – Kilauea erupts almost non-stop.) She also sends out boiling rivers of lava to destroy her enemies. To keep Pele happy (and quiet), people throw offerings into the crater. Could any of these offerings possibly do the trick?

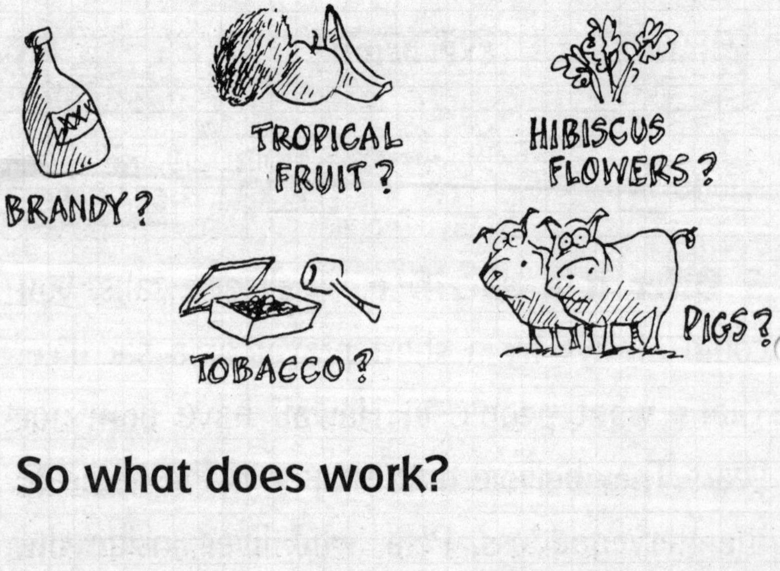

So what does work?

1 Not horribly reliable, but not a bad start. Sometimes it works, but it might burst right through the dam, as happened when Mount Etna erupted in 1983. But four huge barriers (made of volcanic rock and ash) were strong enough to divert the lava away from many important buildings.

2 Not a good idea if you want to keep on friendly terms with the neighbours, the 1669 operation might have saved one town, but it put another town at risk in the process. There was so much quarrelling, a royal decree had to be passed ordering everyone to leave the lava alone, or else!

3 It's a clever idea. This approach has been used several times in Hawaii. In 1935, a lava tube in a flow from Mauna Loa was bombed. The tube was blown apart and became clogged up with chunks of lava, but scientists couldn't tell if the bombing was effective because the eruption went and stopped anyway. In 1942, the same idea was used, but local people got upset, as they thought a bomb would offend Pele, the fire goddess and the only person, as far as they were concerned, who could possibly stop the lava flow. (See page 80 for more details about Pele.)

4 Well, it took weeks ... and weeks ... and weeks. But, in the end, to their immense relief (and great astonishment), their perilous plan worked! At Easter, the lava turned. The front of the flow had cooled fast and hardened, forcing the lava behind it to change direction. Not only was the harbour saved, it was better than ever before. The lava lengthened the harbour wall, giving better protection against the waves. The town was rebuilt and the islanders were able to go back home. A happy ending? Until the next time...

5 OK, so it didn't actually stop the flow, but diverting the lava did save the village of Zafferena which is where the lava was originally heading.

6 They have all been used – but did they work? Well, the brandy was especially effective. When Mauna Loa (another volcano in Pele's charge) erupted in 1881, a lava flow threatened a nearby city. The king's granddaughter was asked to step in. Bold as brass, she stomped straight up to the lava and sprinkled it with a bottle of brandy. And the very next day, it stopped. As for pigs, they're a bit of a love-hate thing. Legend says that Pele almost married Kamapua'a, the pig-man, but it all ended in tears. She told him he was ugly. He put out her fires with fog and rain. The quarrel went on and on. In the end, the gods had to step in and put a stop to it before the whole island was plunged into darkness.

Score one point for each right answer to questions 1–5, and one point for each correct answer in question 6.

Earth-shattering fact

Forget bombs, dams, and bottles of brandy. If you really want to save the day, there's one person who might be able to help ... that's Saint Januarius. He was a bishop in the 3rd century ad who riled the Romans and was thrown to the wild beasts for lunch. But he was so holy that none of the beasts would touch him. Poor old St J was beheaded instead. He later became patron saint of Naples where his skull is kept in a chapel. Except, that is, when Mount Vesuvius looks like erupting. Then it's brought out of hiding and waved in front of the mischievous mountain. Faced with this holy bone, it's said, the volcano goes quiet. At least, it did in 685, 1631 and 1707...

How did you do? Less than four? Well, you know as much as most scientists about volcanoes. Over four, you never know, you might make a brilliant volcanologist. Volcanology isn't all white coats and test-tubes, it's real-life, mind-blowing science…

VIOLENT VOLCANO STUDY

Scientists who study volcanoes are called volcanologists (and yes, they've heard all the jokes about Mr Spock!). All over the world, they're busily trying to get to grips with what makes volcanoes so violent. It's not as easy as it sounds. Studying volcanoes is horribly dangerous. Trickier still is predicting when they might erupt. So why do they do it? Good question. The more we know about volcanoes, the better for everyone. Especially for anyone living near by. Being able to predict eruptions more accurately could save thousands of lives. But the real answer is that, love them or hate them, violent volcanoes are impossible to ignore.

Could you be a vile volcanologist?

Do you have what it takes to become a vile volcanologist? Try this quick quiz to find out.

1 Do you have a head for heights? Yes/No

2 Are you fabulously fit and strong? Yes/No

3 A hot photographer? Yes/No

4 Do you look good in a gas mask? Yes/No

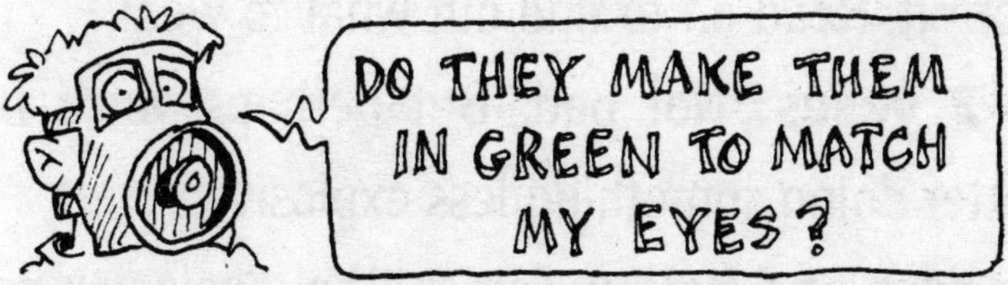

5 Can you tell the date from a tree ring? Yes/No

6 Do you know your rocks? Yes/No

7 Are you fond of travelling? Yes/No

8 Are you good at spelling? Yes/No

9 Are you willing to work odd hours? Yes/No

10 Are you mad? Yes/No

How did you do?

8–10 yeses: Excellent! The job's yours if you want it. Read on to find out what to wear.

5–7 yeses: Not bad. But perhaps you'd be better doing something less explosive.

4 yeses and below: Forget it! Volcanology is not for you. Try something else altogether. Like teaching!

ANSWER

1 You'll need one – some volcanoes are horribly high. It's a very long way up the world's highest active volcano – Guallatiri in Chile's 6,071 metres high. Its last major eruption was in 1987.

2 You'll need to be – there's a lot of hard climbing involved (see above). If you're woefully weak and feeble, you'll never be able to carry all your horribly heavy equipment. Or the even heavier heaps of rock. Time to build those muscles up!

3 Not essential but useful for showing off afterwards.

4 Like it or not, you'll have to wear one. Volcanoes give off lots of gas, most of it horribly poisonous. And collecting gas samples is a major part of your job.

5 Handy if you can. One of a volcanologist's jobs is finding out about past eruptions. Which might give you a clue to a volcano's future. One way of doing this is to look inside a tree. Each year the trunk grows a new ring. It's usually neat and round. But if the tree's been stunted by falling ash, the ring can be horribly thin and wonky.

6 If you can't tell your basalt from your bath salts, you'll be no good to anyone. As every good volcanologist knows basalt is an igneous (fire) rock made when lava cools. And bath salts are things you put in the bath to make you smell better (some hope).

7 It helps. In your quest to get to know a volcano you could be sent anywhere – from icy Antarctica to hot-spot Hawaii.

8 Again, it helps. Some volcanic vocabulary is horribly hard to spell. Take a phreatomagmatic eruption, for example. (Take it very slowly!) To you and me, that's an eruption of gases and steam, with some mega magma thrown in for good measure.

9 No one knows exactly when or where the next volcano is likely to blow. So a good volcanologist has to be ready to leave home at the drop of a (hard) hat.

10 Not compulsory. But it helps. After all, why else would you do a job where you risked being blown up, burned to a crisp, or thrown on the mercy of a feisty fire god?

Dressing the part

If you're going to be a vile volcanologist, you need to dress the part. Safety's more important than looks. Vic is modelling the latest styles in vogue for volcanologists.

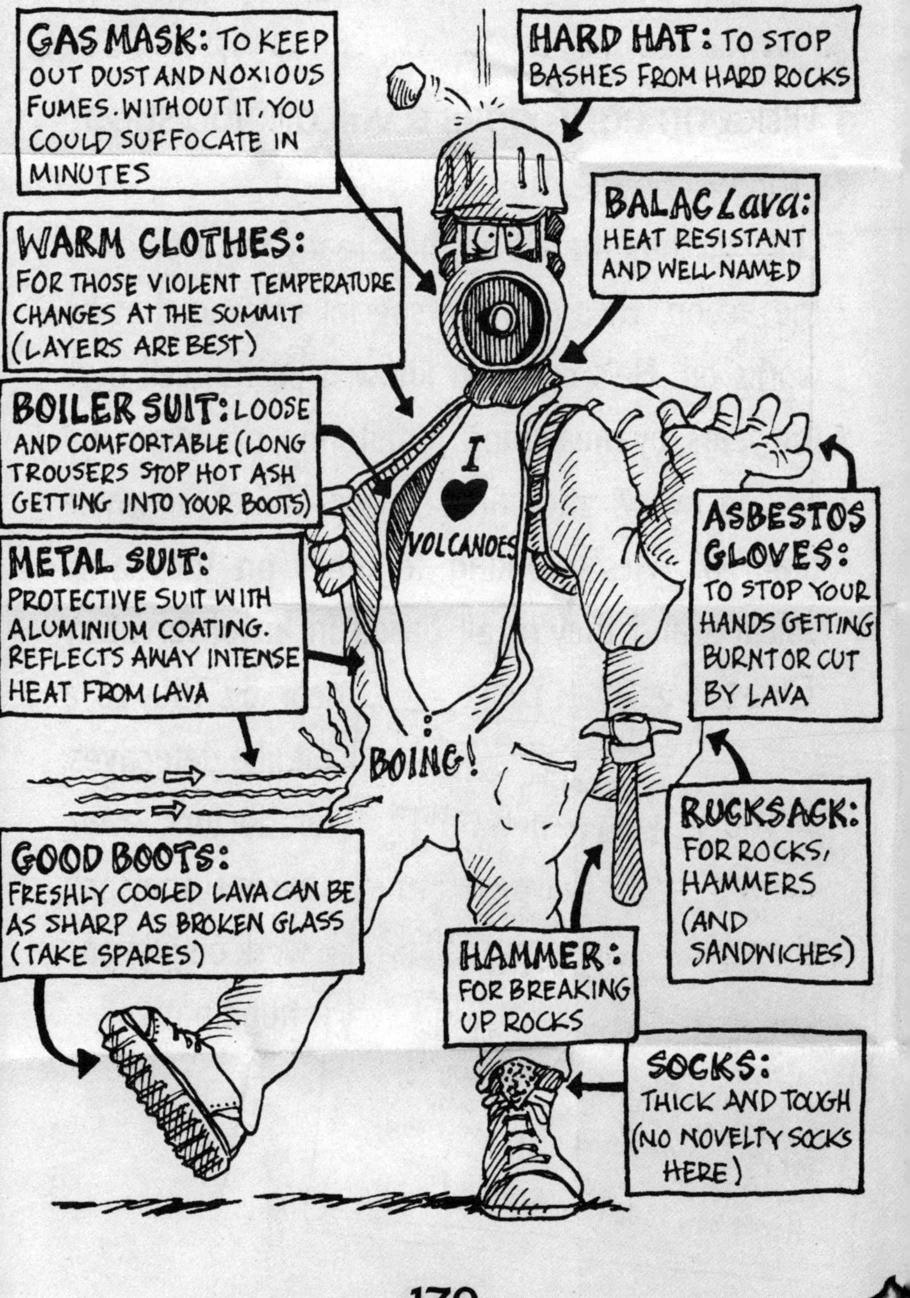
GAS MASK: TO KEEP OUT DUST AND NOXIOUS FUMES. WITHOUT IT, YOU COULD SUFFOCATE IN MINUTES
HARD HAT: TO STOP BASHES FROM HARD ROCKS
BALACLava: HEAT RESISTANT AND WELL NAMED
WARM CLOTHES: FOR THOSE VIOLENT TEMPERATURE CHANGES AT THE SUMMIT (LAYERS ARE BEST)
BOILER SUIT: LOOSE AND COMFORTABLE (LONG TROUSERS STOP HOT ASH GETTING INTO YOUR BOOTS)
I ♥ VOLCANOES
ASBESTOS GLOVES: TO STOP YOUR HANDS GETTING BURNT OR CUT BY LAVA
METAL SUIT: PROTECTIVE SUIT WITH ALUMINIUM COATING. REFLECTS AWAY INTENSE HEAT FROM LAVA
BOING!
RUCKSACK: FOR ROCKS, HAMMERS (AND SANDWICHES)
GOOD BOOTS: FRESHLY COOLED LAVA CAN BE AS SHARP AS BROKEN GLASS (TAKE SPARES)
HAMMER: FOR BREAKING UP ROCKS
SOCKS: THICK AND TOUGH (NO NOVELTY SOCKS HERE)

What on earth does a volcanologist do?

Once Vic has the kit on, he's ready for a piece of the action. He's got one special volcano that he works on. He's come to know it pretty well over the years, by measuring, monitoring, prodding and poking every crack and crevice. There's a whole team of 'Vics' working together on the same volcano and they're all based in an observatory near by. They're a bit like detectives, or doctors, even, except they all work on just one huge patient.

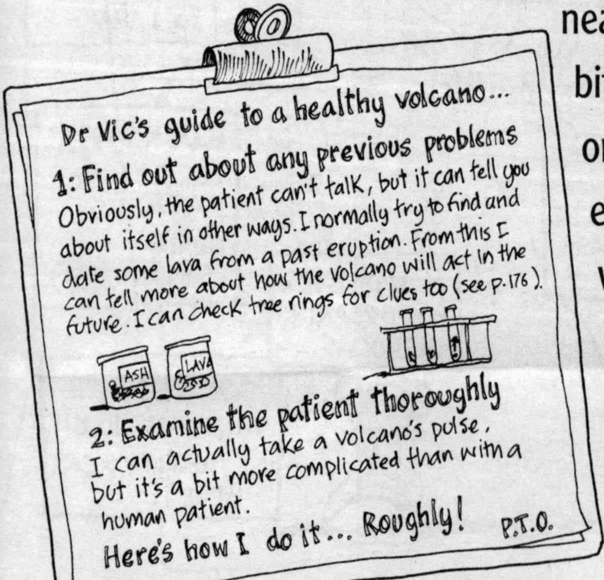

a) Take a couple of gas samples - a volcano gives off more gas just before it erupts.

b) Take its temperature. Mind fingers though - lava can be more than 1,000°C!

c) Feel for bumps or swellings - signs of magma rising up.

d) Listen for any rumblings - these signal earthquakes.

e) Take some samples of lava and rock. I can tell a lot from its age, type and texture.

3: Make your diagnosis

Using all this information I can work out the volcano's 'normal' behaviour. Then I can spot when it starts to act strangely.

4: Find a cure

Ah, yes, this is the difficult bit. So far, no one's come up with a foolproof plan for curing volcanoes of their terrible habit of overflowing. However good your diagnosis, it won't stop the volcano erupting. But you can warn people living nearby to get out of the way... Fast!

Incredible instruments

When you're working with volcanoes, a stethoscope won't be much use, but there are some seriously impressive bits of kit you wouldn't want to leave home without.

1 Seismometer This nifty piece of machinery records the shock waves sent out by earthquakes. Several seismometers are placed around a volcano to measure how often the quakes keep coming, where they're coming from and how big they are. It is also used for detecting lahars.

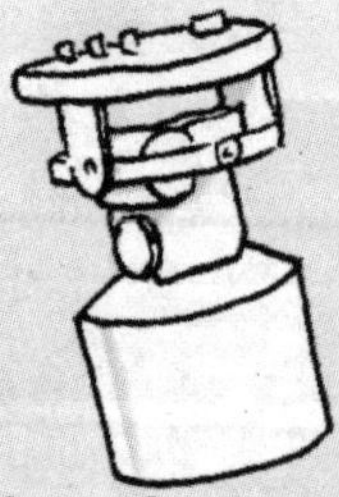

2 Electronic distance meter This measures horizontal ground movements

by shooting out an infrared laser beam. The beam hits a reflector high up on the volcano and bounces back. From the time it takes, vulcanologists can work out if the volcano has budged. It can detect a change of one measly millimetre over 1 kilometre.

3 Electronic tiltmeter This measures vertical ground movements. It's placed in a deep hole drilled as high up on the summit as possible. If the ground shifts, it shifts the fluid in the long tube and sets off an electronic signal.

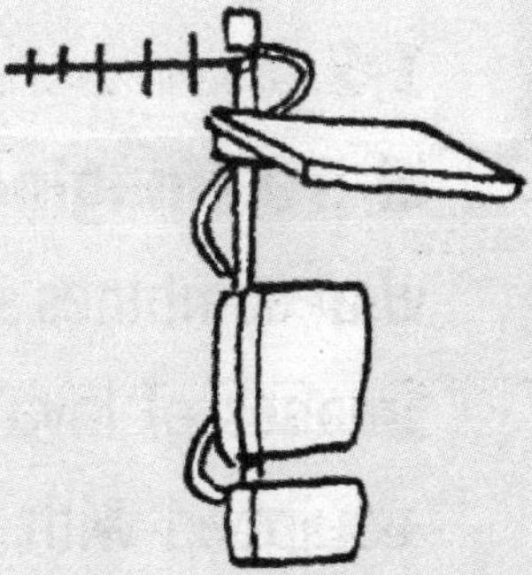

4 Global positioning system (GPS) Satellites beam information to receivers on the volcano so vulcanologists can tell the precise position of ground movements. The same type of system's used in cars for finding the way from A to B.

5 3D imaging This is a very high-tech process that combines satellites with lasers to produce 3D images of lava flows. To collect the data, planes equipped with thousands of lasers fly above the volcano and scan the ground.

6 Correlation spectrometer Used to measure volcanic gases, it's strapped into a car or on to a plane, then driven or flown through a gas plume.

It uses ultraviolet light to measure how much gas is being belched out by the volcano.

7 Thermal imager Special cameras carried by plane or satellite take pictures of the heat a volcano gives off. These 'thermal images' help scientists to spot new (hotter) lava flows and old (cooler ones).

8 Thermocouple A long probe, like a lava thermometer, for measuring lava temperatures. You stick it into the lava, then read the temperature on a hand-held device. Simple as that.

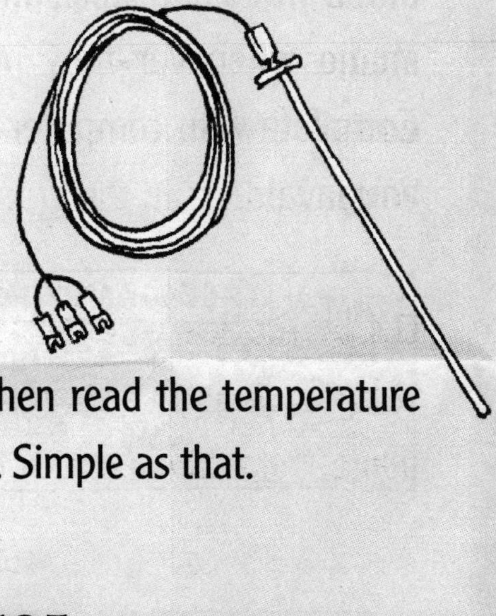

Make your own volcano

If you don't have access to a volcano near you, why not make one of your own? That's what the makers of the film Dante's Peak did. The film tells the story of an active (but make-believe) volcano in the Cascade Mountains, USA. It is about to erupt, any minute. For the starring role, the film-makers built a 10-metre-high model out of wood and steel, and wheeled it out of the studio whenever they needed it for a scene. Complete with computer-generated smoke, ash and lava!

Earth-shattering fact

In 1996, volcanologists in Italy made Mount Vesuvius erupt. On purpose! Why? They said they wanted to see what would happen. They dug 14 holes in the freaky peak's side, then dropped in loads of high explosives. These were blown up by a ship in the bay. BANG! By recording the incredible shock waves from the explosions, the scientists could see what was happening inside. "We want to understand what Vesuvius will be like when it wakes up," said one of the scientists. Weird!

Tragedy at Galeras

Volcanoes can be a bit like people. Just when you think you know them really well, they go and do something quite unexpected.

Violent volcanoes can be especially unpredictable.

Just when you think you've got their number, they can blow up in your face. Several volcanologists are killed every year when the volcanoes they're studying erupt without warning. It's a horribly risky job. Take the tragic events at Galeras, for example.

On 14 January 1993, Galeras volcano in Colombia turned into a killer mountain. A VIP volcano, Galeras was being monitored by a team of volcanologists, led by American scientist, Professor Stan Williams. He had taken a party into the crater to collect gas samples. So far, so good. The volcano was active, and there had been a few small earthquakes but nothing too serious. So the scientists thought. Then things took a turn for the worse. Suddenly, the ground began to rumble and shake and, before the team could get out of harm's way, violent Galeras exploded. In a desperate attempt to save himself, Professor Williams started to run through a rain of rocks bigger than microwave ovens. He didn't make it far. One flying rock broke his skull and jaw. Another smashed both of his legs. His clothes and backpack were set on fire. Slowly and painfully, he crawled inch by inch behind a large boulder and took shelter. Fifteen minutes later, the eruption stopped as suddenly as it began. But it was another two hours before Professor Williams was found, half-dead, and pulled to safety. Despite his horrible injuries, he had had a lucky escape. Three of his colleagues also survived. But six volcanologists and three tourists were killed outright by Galeras's sudden and savage fit of rage.

Professor Williams underwent months of surgery and eventually he was fit enough … to visit the crater of Galeras again.

Some earth-shattering facts about Galeras

1 Galeras is 4,270 metres high and lies just 6 kilometres from the busy city of Pasto in south-western Colombia. Pasto is home to some 300,000 people…

2 …who are in grave danger if the volcano erupts, mainly from pyroclastic flows. For this reason, Galeras was picked as one of the world's 15 VIP volcanoes. It needed watching.

3 Galeras had been dormant until 1988 when it suddenly erupted. It is now classed as an active volcano.

4 Since then, volcanologists have kept a close eye on Galeras. A new observatory has been built and new instruments installed. In future eruptions, the earlier scientists can raise the alarm, the sooner Pasto can be evacuated.

5 Before the explosion, there were a few minor earthquakes but that was nothing to worry about. Two tiltmeters positioned on the volcano's side had showed no change. A fumarole had grown cooler, not hotter, and there was only the slightest trace of gas. Further proof that there was nothing to fear. But, with volcanoes, you never know…

6 Another lesson was learned the hard way. Only one of the group was wearing protective gear. It saved his life. Since then, volcanologists have been better prepared.

7 The volcanologists killed in the tragedy were taking part in an international workshop to study ash, rocks and other debris from past eruptions. They were totally dedicated to their work. Even with such a high price to pay.

Saving lives and false alarms

If volcanologists weren't prepared to risk their lives, then disasters could be even worse. Studying violent volcanoes can save lives. The more scientists know about volcanoes, the earlier they can warn of trouble. If they suspect a volcano is waking up, they can give the order to evacuate ... fast. Any delay could cost lives. Sounds straightforward. But it isn't. Some people don't listen to the scientists' warnings.

Then there's the question of getting it right. Even with the latest in high technology, scientists don't strike lucky every time. Sometimes it's a false alarm. But better to be safe than sorry, they say.

Earth-shattering fact

Scientists monitoring Sakurajima in Japan (another VIP volcano) drilled a tunnel into its side, almost 200 metres long. At the end of the tunnel they placed instruments to measure how much the mountain moved. (Active volcanoes grow and shrink as the pressure inside them builds.) Some of these instruments were so super-sensitive, they could detect the most minuscule movements of the rocks. Even those caused by a single person walking down the tunnel! Awesome. Now, after years and years of careful study, scientists can warn the locals that Sakurajima is set to strike... a full 20 seconds before it happens!

Getting it wrong

Things don't always go according to plan. When Nevado del Ruiz in Colombia erupted in November 1985, a lethal lahar completely demolished the nearby town of Armero. Almost 25,000 people died as waves of mud 40 metres high simply swept Armero away. Ten thousand more lost their homes. Although only a tenth as violent as the eruption of Mount St Helens, it was the greatest volcanic disaster of the century, second only to Mount Pelée in terms of lives lost. (About 30,000 people died when Mount Pelée blew.) The tragedy was, it needn't have been. Scientists warned the government officials what to expect. But they didn't take them seriously. They claimed they couldn't run the risk that it might turn out to be a false alarm. In the event, the eruption began at 3 pm on the afternoon of 13 November. By evening, despite a meeting of the emergency committee, no evacuation plans had been made. By the time they had been, it was too late. At 9 pm, Nevado del Ruiz began to belch out pyroclastic flows which melted part of its ice cap. A lethal lahar of water and ash raced downhill at speeds of up to 40 kilometres an hour. Two hours later, it hit Armero. It was too late for anyone to get out of its way.

Getting it right

Which makes getting it right even sweeter. When Mount Pinatubo in the Philippines erupted violently in 1991, scientific know-how saved thousands of lives. One of the biggest eruptions of the 20th century, it came right out of the blue – the volcano hadn't murmured in living memory. Ash, lahars and pyroclastic flows devastated the surrounding countryside. Tens of thousands of people lived on or near the volcano. Over a thousand died and 2.1 million people were affected, many losing their homes and livelihood. But, believe it or not, it could have been worse. A whole lot worse. The scientists acted fast. At the first sign of trouble, they evacuated everyone living within 10 kilometres of the summit. Then, using a network of portable seismographs, they monitored the volcano day and night. A hazard map showing possible danger zones was quickly drawn up. This time officials and public alike followed the scientists' early warnings that Pinatubo was about to erupt. A video was shown, explaining the dangers but without all the tedious technical terms. The video alone saved thousands of lives – at least people knew what to do. Even so, they only just made it. On 12 June, the evacuation zone was extended to 30 kilometres and 35,000 people were forced to flee their homes. Just in time. Three days later, on 15 June, at 6 am, Pinatubo blew apart. An eruption cloud 20 kilometres high spread out like a skirt around the volcano. Pyroclastic flows snaked 16 kilometres from the summit. Lahars spilled over and covered the countryside. But, at least the volcano doctors had got it right.

Even so, they can't take all the credit. In fact, the first inkling scientists had that Pinatubo was stirring came from a passing nun. She walked into the Philippine Institute of Volcanology and told the stunned scientists the volcano was smoking! And she was right!

Today, predicting volcanoes is getting easier all the time. But it's still not an exact science. Violent volcanoes are horribly mysterious. And constantly changing. Which proves a real headache for the steamed-up scientists. Is the volcano about to blow? Or not? Should they order an evacuation? Or not? What if the volcano's calling their bluff? And many, many more vexing questions besides. And even if you can predict an eruption, there's nothing you can do to stop it. Absolutely nothing at all.

NOT-SO-VIOLENT VOLCANOES?

Like them or loathe them, violent volcanoes are here to stay. We'll just have to learn to live with them. And everyone or everything has their good points. Don't they? Even violent volcanoes. OK, so you wouldn't want one in your back garden (like poor Farmer Pulido and peaky Parícutin). But they do have their uses.

Here are some of the things you wouldn't have if there weren't any violent volcanoes.

Without violent volcanoes, you'd miss out on…

1 The odious oceans Believe it or not, it was violent volcanoes that created the oceans and seas. To find out how, you need to travel back in time some 4,600 million years to the early days on Earth. Things looked very different then. Our brand-new planet was covered with thousands of volcanoes. Which never slept. As they erupted, they shot out streams of water vapour – a steamy gas. This cooled and formed storm clouds full of rain. The rain fell, filled the oceans and hey presto! Water also gushed up from underground. The oceans, however, weren't like the salty seas we know today. They were boiling hot, awesomely acidic and full of colourful chemicals. Not exactly the perfect holiday spot.

2 The awesome atmosphere The early Earth was an eerie place. For one thing, it had no atmosphere. Violent volcanoes changed all that. Over millions of years, they belched out gases – mostly steamy water vapour, colourless carbon dioxide and stinky sulphur dioxide. It wasn't an atmosphere as we know it. For one thing, you couldn't have breathed it in – it didn't have any oxygen. (This had to wait for plants to come along. They release oxygen when they make their food. But that's another story...) But it was certainly better than nothing.

3 Life itself That's about as useful as you can get. To tell the truth, volcanoes didn't actually create life themselves. But they created the right conditions for it. Life is thought to have begun in the odiously early oceans. The first living things were tiny bacteria which grew about 3,500 million years ago. How do we know? Scientists have found fossils of some of them in ancient rocks. They didn't need oxygen to live (there wasn't any, so it was just as well). Instead, they gobbled up chemicals from the hot soupy seas, especially nitrogen and sulphur which came out of violent volcanoes. A German scientist, who dedicated his life to studying weird wildlife, claims their descendants are still alive and well. They thrive around hot volcanic springs and volcanic vents in the sea floor. They also live in pools of oil, sulphur springs and rubbish heaps. As long as it's hot, steaming and smells terrible, they feel at home!

4 Monster mountains Some of the greatest mountains on Earth were built by violent volcanoes. Take the awesome Andes, for example. They run for more than 7,000 kilometres along the west coast of South America – the longest mountain chain in the world. This is where one plate (the one that carries the Pacific Ocean) is dipping under another (the one that carries South America). As the lower plate plunges down, it gets horribly hot and starts to melt. Then the molten magma rises up through the upper plate, triggering off violent volcanoes.

5 Flaming islands Many islands are in fact volcanoes – Iceland, Hawaii, Tristan da Cunha, the gorgeous Galapagos to name a few. They're actually the tips of underwater volcanoes, which have grown tall enough to keep their heads above water. There are thousands of volcanoes under the sea, all at least a kilometre tall. They've been built up over millions of years by lava creeping up through the crust. And they're still growing. As this story shows…

Happy birthday, Surtsey

No one had ever seen a volcanic island grow. That is, until November 1963. Then, early one morning, some fishermen off the coast of Iceland had the greatest surprise of their lives. As they watched, the sea began to smoke and steam, hissing like a kettle. At first, the fishermen thought a boat had caught fire. But when they got closer, they saw that the sea itself

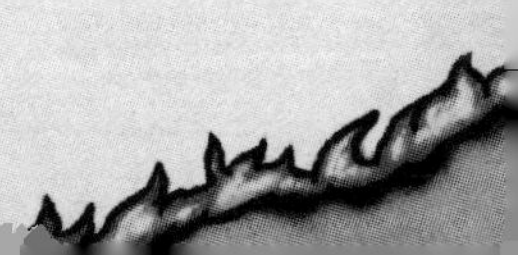

was boiling and bubbling. A violent volcano was coming up for air!

By next day, an island had been born. After they'd recovered from the shock, nearby islanders called it Surtsey, after their ancient god of fire. When it stopped erupting about three years later, Surtsey measured about 2.5 square kilometres, about as big as 230 football pitches. It was bare and black. But not for long. Within just a few months, the first plants began to grow from seeds carried there by birds or the wind. More seeds, and birds, followed. Four years later, the island was thriving.

Over a hot spot under the Pacific, not far from Hawaii, a brand-new island is starting to grow. Called Loihi, it's already 2,700 metres tall. Only another 1,000 metres to go until it pokes up out of the sea. Hawaii's actually a chain of 100 volcanoes. Some have now sunk back beneath the waves. Little Loihi will be the youngest in the family (ages range from an ancient 80 million years old to a measly one million years old). Scientists are already getting horribly excited and are keeping a very close eye on Loihi, sending down cameras and submarines. They're in for a very long wait. It'll be at least another 60,000 years before Loihi pops its fiery head above the windswept waves.

And there's something else lurking beneath those waves, it's the one bit of Hawaii that isn't volcanic...

6 Collapsing coral An atoll is a tiny ring-shaped island constructed of coral around a deep blue lagoon. You'll find them in warm, tropical seas. Lovely! But what have they got to do with volcanoes? Here's what.

The first person to work this out was the brilliant British scientist, Charles Darwin (1809–1882). (Darwin was famous for discovering that horrible humans are descended from apes.) At the time, it was only a guess. Over a hundred years later, a team of scientists on Bikini Atoll in the Pacific were studying the effects of an atom bomb test. They drilled some holes into the atoll and found that the coral was indeed resting on volcanic rock. Darwin had got it right.

7 Famous landmarks Many of the world's most famous landmarks are volcanic. Take the Giant's Causeway in Northern Ireland, for example. It's made of hundreds of huge, hexagonal blocks and pillars of basalt formed millions of years ago when a volcano cooled. (There are no active volcanoes in Ireland today.) It's called a causeway because some of the rocks look rather like stepping stones, stretching six kilometres along the coast. Legend says that it was once a pathway for giants popping over to Scotland for a visit.

A violent future?

Violent volcanoes have been around for a very long time. And they're not going to go away. So what on earth does the future hold?

VIP volcanoes

At present, scientists are monitoring about half of the world's 550 active land volcanoes. Closely.

Another 300 need careful watching. Sixteen VIP volcanoes have been singled out for special study. They're the freakiest peaks in the world. And the most urgent to understand. You might have heard of some of them before… The modern world has never experienced a truly massive volcanic eruption. The last VEI 8 explosion was 75,000 years ago. But another one may soon be due. Horrible geographers reckon on two VEI 8s every 100,000 years. Some warn that a 'Big One' is already overdue.

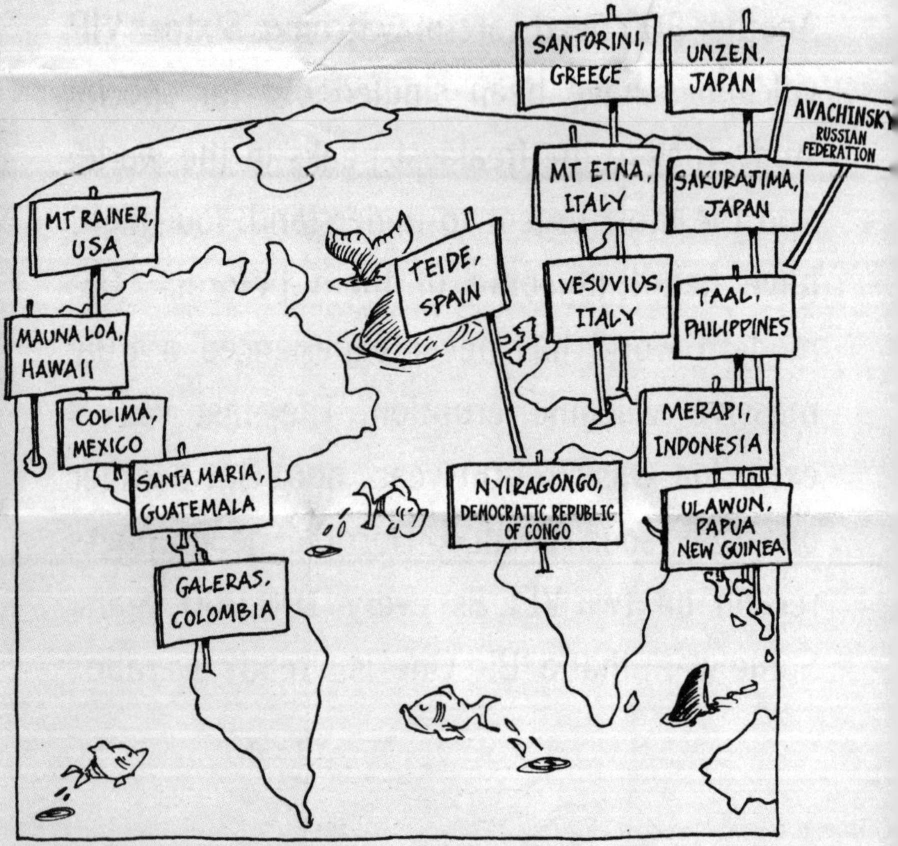

And it wouldn't be a pretty sight. The ashy aftermath

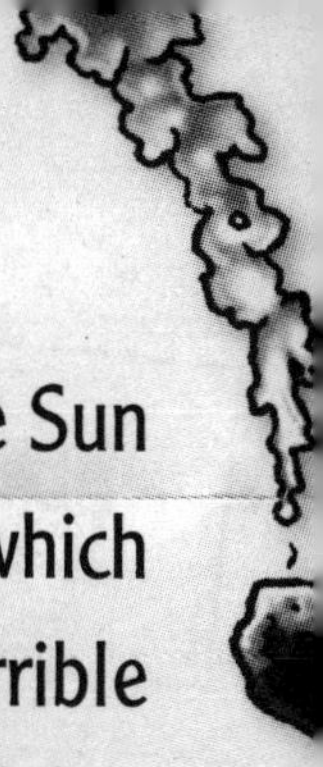

of a really BIG explosion would blot out the Sun for years on end. No Sun means no plants which means NO FOOD. Now there's a horrible thought. So should we be worried? Are we living on borrowed time? What if the Big One happens soon? Before you start work on your volcano shelter, don't forget – 'soon' to a scientist doesn't mean today, tomorrow, or even next week, they're more likely talking 25,000 years away…

HORRIBLE INDEX

MORE HORRIBLE GEOGRAPHY ADVENTURES TO EXPLORE!

HORRIBLE GEOGRAPHY
ODIOUS
OCEANS
ANITA GANERI ILLUSTRATED BY MIKE PHILLIPS

HORRIBLE GEOGRAPHY
RAGING RIVERS
ANITA GANERI ILLUSTRATED BY MIKE PHILLIPS

HORRIBLE GEOGRAPHY
BLOOMIN' RAINFORESTS
ANITA GANERI ILLUSTRATED BY MIKE PHILLIPS

HORRIBLE GEOGRAPHY
STORMY WEATHER
ANITA GANERI ILLUSTRATED BY MIKE PHILLIPS

HORRIBLE GEOGRAPHY
STOP
EARTH-SHATTERING EARTHQUAKES
ANITA GANERI ILLUSTRATED BY MIKE PHILLIPS